Cooking for Dogs

Nutrition Guide for Healthy Dogs

Easy, All-Natural Meal and Treat Recipes for Dogs of All Ages

Lou Jefferson

Copyrights

All rights reserved. © Lou Jefferson and Maplewood Publishing. No part of this publication or the information in it may be quoted from or reproduced in any form by means such as printing, scanning, photocopying, or otherwise without prior written permission of the copyright holder.

Disclaimer and Terms of Use

Effort has been made to ensure that the information in this book is accurate and complete. However, the author and the publisher do not warrant the accuracy of the information, text, and graphics contained within the book due to the rapidly changing nature of science, research, known and unknown facts, and internet. The author and the publisher do not hold any responsibility for errors, omissions, results using the information in this book or contrary interpretation of the subject matter herein. Consider all information in this book to be for entertainment purposes and not professional advice, and to be used at your own risk. The author and publisher of this book cannot be held responsible for the consequences of your actions and it is understood that you will use the information in accordance to the laws of your own country. This book is presented solely for motivational, entertainment and informational purposes only.

Contents

Introduction _____ 1
What to Feed Your Dog: the Options _____ 3
What Should Be in a Dog Diet? _____ 23
Treats and Supplements _____ 37
Through the Ages: Puppies and Older Dogs _____ 46
Dogs with Special Medical Conditions _____ 53
Dogs with Allergies and Sensitivities _____ 52
Recipes for Growing Puppies _____ 61
Recipes for Full Grown Dogs _____ 81
Recipes for Lactating Dogs _____ 101
Vegetarian Dog Food Recipes _____ 123
Dog Treat Recipes _____ 127
Quick and Easy Dog Treat Recipes _____ 130
Gourmet Dog Food Recipes _____ 137
Parting Words _____ 141
Also by Lou Jefferson _____ 143

Introduction

Are you having difficulty finding the perfect meal for your dog? Do you have doubts about the nutritional content of the commercially sold dog food in the market? Are you in search of new, delicious, and easy-to-cook dog food recipes for your dog? Now you don't have to worry about that anymore, because this book contains everything you need to know about dog food recipes and more. No more searching – the answer to your problem is now in your hands. All you've got to do is take this book home with you and get started.

Since everything from the environment, to genetics, and pollution can to affect the health of our dogs, one way we can ensure that they can fight back against possible diseases is by giving them the right kind of food. Food that is not just healthy, but also suitable for their daily needs. It may sound impossible, but after you read this book, you'll see a whole new world not just for you as a dog lover, but for your dog as well. For dog food cannot just be chosen at random. You have to have the necessary information to ensure that what you are giving to your dog is good for his health.

One of the most common assumptions that dog owners make is that as long as they feed their dogs and walk them every day, they'll be healthy. But little do they know, right? Because just like us human beings, our dogs also require the proper nutrients and a balanced diet in order to live well. Aside from grooming and exercise, healthy food is also important for our dogs to grow to their full potential.

From now on, you can say goodbye to your many doubtful moments in the supermarket, wondering which dog food product to choose. And instead of just buying a commercial dog food, you'll be able to buy your own ingredients and then make the dog food yourself. What better way to serve your dog his meal than with one you have prepared yourself? However, you do need to be cautious, because cooking your meals is different from cooking your dog's. There are many things you should consider – not just the process, but the ingredients as well.

That's why this book will be your ultimate buddy in the kitchen, if you choose you prepare your dog's personal menu for his daily meals. So gear up and buy as many ingredients as you like, because for the coming days you just might be busy reading and cooking. Say goodbye to synthetic ingredients and welcome the upcoming days of cooking healthy and delicious dog foods. Now, I know that you are very excited to start cooking for your dog, let's get started!

What to Feed Your Dog: the Options

In this day and age it seems that dog owners are putting out a great effort when it comes to feeding their dogs the proper food for better health and longevity. The question then arises – what *should* you feed your dog? Is organic dog food the better choice? What about raw food? Can dogs be vegetarians? These are great questions, and there are many opinions on the subject. We've provided many of the answers in this book.

Ultimately, your decision will most likely will come down to your personal lifestyle and preferences. What works for you and your dog could be vastly different from what other people do, but the important thing is to consider the matter and make an informed choice.

There are four main options for feeding your dog, once he is fully grown: commercial food (dry or wet), a natural diet, a vegetarian diet, or a mixture of these.

What You Need to Know About Commercial food

There have been many tainted pet food scandals in the news in recent years, and so the public's faith in getting a consistently safe product from the major dry dog food manufacturers has been severely shaken. In addition, dry food is full of fillers: corn meal, bone meal, and worse, soy meal. These don't contribute much to the welfare of our beloved pets, and in fact they can have negative effects. For an older dog, these fillers mean larger and sometimes painful bowel movements, and an inefficient transfer of nutrients to the dog's system. As vulnerable as these products are to molds and other contaminants, they are generally a bad choice. Even supplemented with vitamins, fish oil, and velvet antler, this diet is has little to offer your dog, especially if she is older.

Wet food, usually in a can or packet, is better by far for safety; the packaging is nearly impervious to contamination. The main weakness of these dog foods is that they are very high in preservatives, another ingredient your dog can do without. Wet food, with its higher water content is easier, however, for them to digest.

Many agree that when using commercial foods, a combination of wet and dry is best for your dog.

Dog Food Ingredients

Commercial dog food companies are in a mad dash to get a dominant chunk of this lucrative market. In an attempt to entice and convince dog owners that their product is the best for pets, manufacturers are incorporating unconventional dog food ingredients in the food, in addition to the usual things. It's not unusual to find misleading marketing strategies, and we have no way to substantiate many of the claims being made.

Quality pet food should be formulated with the dog's daily nutrient requirements in mind. It should be noted that your dog's different life stages have different nutritional requirements. Thus, it is very important that food for your dog should be intended for his age.

You might have observed that commercial rations for puppies are priced higher than those marketed for adult dogs. The amount of the protein component of the food usually dictates the price. Since puppies and growing dogs need more protein, and protein sources are quite expensive, their food is inevitably priced higher.

In an effort to cut overhead costs and make more profit, there are manufacturers that use meat substitutes and fillers. These dog food ingredients are definitely substandard, and subsequently fail in fulfilling the required nutrient intake. To make matters worse, meat substitutes such as meat by-products have been linked to various health problems in dogs.

As a responsible dog owner, you should know how to read and interpret the composition and/or ingredients of pet food products. Many manufacturers have been adding unusual dog food ingredients that may be harmful to your dog. Some of the most common ingredients you might notice listed in dog food labels include additives, binders, carbohydrate sources, coloring agents, fiber sources, flavoring agents, and fruits and vegetables (from unhealthy origins).

Additives
The most common additives include Glyceryl Monostearate, Phosphoric acid, and Propylene Glycol.

- **Glyceryl Monostearate** is an emulsifier commonly used in the foodstuff industry. It can contain butylated hydroxytoluene (BHT) of more than 200 ppm.
- **Phosphoric Acid** is often used as flavoring and emulsifying agent of inferior quality dog food.
- **Propylene Glycol** is added to prevent semi-moist kibble from drying out. It can be toxic when added in large quantities. Countries under the European Union have not approved propylene glycol as a food additive.

Binders
Binders that you commonly see in dog food products include corn gluten and wheat gluten. These ingredients have been linked to a major percentage of food allergies in dogs. Gluten meals are inexpensive by-products with low nutritional value.

Carbohydrate Sources
Brewer's rice has been used by manufacturers as a low-quality and inexpensive substitute for whole grain rice. Other non-desirable carbohydrate feed sources which are often added to pet food rations include grain fermentation soluble, cereal foods, oat meal, maltodextrins, soy flour, and potato peels and culls.

As you can see, these are mostly by-products of human food processing and consequently do not have desirable nutritional values.

Coloring Agents
Color additives are known carcinogens. Cases of allergic reactions that have been linked to food coloring have also been recorded in dogs. The most common coloring agents found in pet foods include Blue 2, Red 40, titanium dioxide, Yellow 5, and Yellow 6.

Flavoring Agents
The flavoring agents commonly found in pet food products include animal digest such as lamb digest, chicken digest, or poultry liver digest. Most of these ingredients likely come from animal tissues of "4-D animals" (diseased, disabled, dying, or dead).

Fiber Sources
A dog's digestive system is not designed for the efficient digestion of fibrous feed ingredients. Although fiber is needed in small quantities for its cleansing effect on the digestive tract, high amounts of fibrous ingredients in dog food is not desirable. Many pet food manufacturers incorporate fiber sources to add consistency and bulk to poor quality food. A few of the common fiber sources you can find in dog food ingredients include corn bran, cellulose, oat hulls, peanut hulls, wheat mill run, and soybean mill run.

Fruits and Vegetables
Fruits and vegetables are good sources of vitamins and minerals, however most of those used as a dog food ingredient are by-products of processing. They are also a likely source of residues from synthetic fertilizers and pesticides. Some fruits, such as grapes, also contain a substance which is toxic to dogs.

A responsible dog owner is a vigilant dog owner. Take the time to get to know a pet food product by reading the fine lines of the ingredients. The key that can unlock the mystery of whether a particular product is the best one for your dog is to know the dog food ingredients that make up the product.

The Case for Organic Commercial Food
If you decide to feed your pet commercial food, **a brand like Holistic Select®** might be a good choice. We'll go over the benefits of this one brand, so you can use the rationale to assess other foods that are available.

What's in it?
Lamb, tuna, salmon, shrimp, chicken, liver, and duck – you might only expect to see these ingredients in a kitchen for a chef to

prepare a sumptuous human dinner. But you can also find them in the various formulas and recipes of Holistic Select® dog food.

This brand of pet nutrition offers dry and canned formulas of a good range of recipes to suit the different needs of your dogs. Among its popular healthy recipes are Adult Lamb Meal; Adult Duck Meal; Tuna, Salmon, and Shrimp canned food; and Chicken and Chicken Liver canned food.

Their Adult Lamb Meal contains lamb as its premium protein source. Lamb is a preferred meat, because it is hypoallergenic and tasty compared to poultry. Lamb meat included in this recipe comes from the striated muscle that's either skeletal or found in the heart or tongue. It may or may not include the fat and parts of the skin, nerve, sinew, and blood vessels that usually go with this type of meat. It also has taurine, which is good for your pet's eyes and heart. To boost your dog's immune system and minimize cell deterioration, antioxidants like beta-carotene and vitamins A, C, and E are also added to the product.

The Holistic Select® dog food Adult Duck Meal variation, as the name says, has duck as its prime protein-rich ingredient. Compared to chicken, duck is tastier and higher in protein content. This recipe also contains oatmeal, rice, and organic quinoa, which is a top-quality grain. Organic quinoa is not only hypoallergenic, but also easily digestible, making it a safe ingredient for your dogs. This ingredient makes the Adult Duck Meal recipe high in calcium, iron, B vitamins, and phosphorus.

The Tuna, Salmon, and Shrimp canned dog food by Holistic Select® has yummy seafood, plus oat bran. Salmon in this recipe is cooked to release excess fat and water, and come up with an easily digestible meal that's rich in not only protein, but also calcium and long-chain Omega-3 fatty acids. These elements contribute to the health of the body, skin, and coat.

The brand also has Chicken and Chicken Liver canned dog food, which is another source of high-quality protein and vitamins A, B, and D for your pet. It even has yucca schidigera extract, which can naturally help your pet's joint health. It also aids in the reduction of urine and fecal odor.

The most important thing to remember is that adult dogs need enough nutrients to supply the energy they need, and to maintain and repair their body tissues. The amount of nutrition an adult dog needs all depends on the output of energy, level of activity, and their size as well. Once you know the amount of energy he requires, you can adjust the portions of food you give him every day.

Another factor you should consider when feeding your adult dog is the temperature. Sometimes extreme heat or cold will cause your dog to have varying energy needs, and it is a best practice to consult with your vet to make sure you are using the best type of food and a feeding schedule that is suitable.

Although not all of these solutions address the current safety problems associated with commercial dog food, they do help to provide a working nutritional solution for your canine friend.

A Natural Diet – or Raw Feeding

A natural diet takes more effort than either dry or canned commercial food, but it has numerous benefits ranging from the best nutrition value to being the easiest to digest. If pre-prepared in a once-a-week effort, most of the work is removed. Recipes for these diets abound on the internet – hundreds of sites include recipes based on chicken, veal, and beef diets, including several recipes for wild game such as elk and deer. Supplemented with greens, fish oil, and velvet antler for arthritic joints, this method offers the most for most dogs. We also provide many good recipes in this book, for dogs of all ages.

You may judge the natural diet as too much work, despite its obvious advantages. In such a case, they consider combining a few elements of a natural diet with a wet or dry food regimen to relieve some of the stress from your dog's digestive system, and lengthen his life.

Remember to talk with your veterinarian before making any major changes to your pet's diet.

Tips for Feeding Your Dog Raw Meat

1. Do Your Research First

The first thing you need to do is get your facts straight and make sure you understand what indeed is good or bad for your pet. Get a sense of what kinds of ingredients you'll need to have on hand, and what to avoid. Much of the required information is here in this book. Figure out how much raw meat your dog should be eating, based on the breed, size, and type of animal he is. This is a big change for you and your pet so you need to be fully prepared. A gradual transition is best.

The first thing you are going to want to look at is what types of meats are safe for dogs to eat. Dogs are often fed beef, chicken, pork, venison, rabbit, and other game. Birds are great for dogs as well. If you are ever unsure than it is best to wait and find out if it is safe first.

Many people feel that large bones are indeed safe for dogs to eat, and they are very important for dental health, however, they need to be raw. If you feed your dog cooked bones you are asking for a disaster. Meat and bones that are fed to dogs always need to be raw. Cooked bones can splinter and cooked meats are hard on a dog's digestive system. Veterinarians want us to know that even with raw bones, there are instances of damages like wounds and punctures in a dog's mouth and digestive system. You need to decide for yourself how you feel about that risk, and always keep an eye on your dog when she is chewing a bone. Be sure to take it away if it is disintegrating.

2. Switching Your Dog to Raw Meat

The hardest part of all of this is making the change to your dog's diet. Some dogs will automatically switch over gracefully while others won't even touch the new food you are giving them. The easiest way to deal with picky eaters is to find a gateway meat. Most dogs will have one type of meat they find attractive over everything else. Try finding your dog beef, and if he doesn't like it, then try chicken.

Adult dogs should be fed at a minimum of 18% protein and 5% fat, and you should be aware of the proportion of protein and fat required. If you add oil to make his food tastier, then you should include additional sources of protein or supplements in order to make sure your dog is well nourished. Try to introduce at least a new recipe every month, and do not feed your dog the same monotonous meal all the time.

Commercial raw food packaging has serving size suggestions on the wrapping, so this might be a good place to start. Usually you offer food in the amount of 2-3% of your dog's ideal body weight per day, and this should consist of meat, fruits and vegetables, bones, and organs, in that order of decreasing proportion.

How much you feed your dog depends on the dog, and it is the dog owner's responsibility to discover how much homemade food his dog needs. Two dogs of the same size and breed with the same level of mental and physical activity will not necessarily require the same quantity of food. Keep an eye on your dog, looking for any increase or decrease in body weight or energy level, and adjust the food amount accordingly. If the dog's coat becomes dull, or his bowel movements difficult, then you may need to add more fat or more fiber. If you observe something strange you should immediately stop the food you think may be the cause, and see if things go back to normal.

3. How Much to Feed your Dog Raw Food per Day

Here's a table based on the dogs' weight that you can use as a starting point:

Body weight kg/lbs		2.5kg / 5.5lbs	5kg / 11lbs	10kg / 22lbs	15kg / 33lbs
Protein	Meat	30 - 37.5gr	60 - 75gr	120 - 150gr	180 - 225gr
	Bones	5 - 7.5gr	10 - 15gr	20 - 30gr	30 - 45gr
	Organs	2.5 - 5gr	5 - 10gr	10 - 20gr	15 - 30gr
Veggies & Fruits		7.5 - 12.5gr	15 - 25gr	30 - 50gr	45 - 75gr
Total (2% of body weight)		50gr	100gr	200gr	300gr
Body weight kg/lbs		20kg / 44lbs	25kg / 55.1lbs	30kg / 66.1lbs	35kg / 77.1lbs
Protein	Meat	240 - 300gr	300 - 375gr	360 - 450gr	420 - 525gr
	Bones	40 - 60 gr	50 - 75gr	30 - 60gr	70 - 105gr
	Organs	20 - 40gr	25 - 50gr	60 - 90gr	35 - 70gr
Veggies & Fruits		60 - 100gr	75 - 125gr	90 - 150	105 - 175gr
Total (2% of body weight)		400gr	500gr	600gr	700gr

Body weight kg/lbs		40kg / 88.2lbs	45kg / 99.2lbs	50kg / 110.2lbs
Protein	Meat	480 - 600gr	540 - 675gr	600 - 750gr
	Bones	80 - 120gr	90 - 135gr	100 - 150gr
	Organs	40 - 80gr	45 - 90gr	50 - 100gr
Veggies & Fruits		120 - 200gr	135 - 225gr	150 - 250gr
Total (2% of body weight)		800gr	900gr	1kg

Pros and Cons of the Raw Dog Food Diet

The popularity of the raw food diet for dogs is increasing as dog owners look for alternatives to mass-produced commercial dog foods. The general theory is that by feeding raw, natural, organic foodstuffs, the overall diet is less reliant on fillers, chemicals, and additives, and there is more emphasis on what the animal would eat naturally. As a result, the dog should be healthier and happier. That said, there are both pros and cons to such a dietary approach. Let's take a look at some of them and how the cons may be combatted.

Pro: If you start to use the raw food diet your dog may develop a shiner coat. In general, dog food products sold in stores do not contain all the nutrients that the animal needs. One of the key nutrients that you will not find in food products is the oil which helps to promote that shiny coat. The raw foods contain such nutrients, giving your pet a healthier coat.

Pro: If you would like your dog to have more energy, avoid processed food. This is because the dog's body needs more time to metabolize the commercial food. The raw food can be digested more easily. This means that the dog's body can readily extract energy from raw food, and this translates to higher energy levels.

Pro: The raw dog food diet helps clean and toughen the dog's teeth, especially when you give him bones to chew on. The teeth rub against the bone as he chews on it. The rubbing cleans his teeth and strengthens both the gums and teeth against decay.

Con: Raw meat contains bacteria which may cause sickness for the dog or humans who handle the food. Harmful bacteria, if ingested, can cause many kinds of issues for your dog, just like in humans. To combat this, always buy quality fresh meat from sources you can trust, such as your local butcher. If you're buying commercial raw food, (or making your own ahead of time) make sure it's frozen until the day before you use it, and clean the dog's dishes thoroughly.

Con: As the dog chews on bones, slivers may break off. This can result in punctures in your dog's organs. Bones can also potentially crack the teeth, making it painful for your dog to eat and resulting in a hefty vet bill. Always consider this when giving your dog a bone. Stick to large, meaty bones, and never give cooked bones to a dog.

Con: When you feed your dog a raw food diet, you must be sure to supplement where necessary with other nutrients and vitamins to provide an overall balanced diet. If you feed the dog raw food only, and for a prolonged period of time, he may experience deficiencies, leading to problems that could become serious. Ensuring a balanced diet that includes bone, organ meat, and fruits and vegetables is very important, so your dog will be happier and healthier.

Now you have a view of some of the advantages and disadvantages of introducing your dog to a different diet while still maintaining the overall importance of nutritional balance for his health. **A raw diet might not suit all dogs so it is suggested that if you are in any doubt, talk to your vet.**

Vegetarian Diet

Vegetarian diets can be very healthy for humans, and many people think that a meatless diet could provide the same kind of benefits to their dog. If you're considering putting your dog on a vegetarian diet, there are a number of things you'll need to think about.

While you can buy vegetarian pet foods at your local store, vegetarian dog diets are extremely controversial. Many believe that a dog isn't able to get all of the nutrients it needs without meat. In nature, they eat mainly meat. Dogs don't process nutrients in the same ways humans do, and they may miss out on some important vitamins and minerals if they stop eating meat.

One of the things that dogs need to have in their diet is taurine. Dogs are only able to produce taurine if they're fed the right types of protein, and the easiest source of this protein is meat products.

Dogs are also unable to produce Vitamin D on their own, which means that they need to consume foods that provide it. A dog can get Vitamin D without eating meat, but it can be a challenge. If you do decide to switch over to a vegetarian dog food, you'll need to make sure it provides your dog with both of these things.

A dog also needs a lot more protein than a human in order to stay healthy. It's recommend that dogs consume at least 25 grams of protein for every 1000 calories they eat. If your dog isn't eating meat, this can be very hard to achieve.

Other vitamins and minerals that vegetarian dog food may be deficient in include calcium, B vitamins, amino acids, and iron. There are other animal products that contain these things, which means a vegetarian diet can work for a dog, but a vegan one can't.

If a dog's diet doesn't have all the nutrients he needs, it can cause some very serious health problems. For example, a poor diet can lead to heart problems and even heart failure. In some cases, an unhealthy diet has proven to be fatal.

A vegetarian diet for a dog is risky, and you'll need to be very careful if you decide to do it. You should make sure you bring up the diet with your veterinarian and address any concerns they might have. You should also make sure that you feed your dog a commercial dog food from a respected brand rather than making your own meals.

In some situations, a vegetarian diet will be the healthiest choice for a dog. For example, your dog may have a food allergy. If this is the case, your vet will be able to give your dog a prescription dog food that addresses those problems.

A vegetarian diet isn't ideal for a dog, but it can be done. You just need to make sure that you're cautious and careful so your dog can remain healthy. You don't want your dog's diet to put him at risk.

Common Misconceptions about Dog Food

Preparing homemade meals for our pets is a healthier alternative to buying even premium ready-made products available at the market. The difficult part is selecting the right ingredients and alternatives to them. These take careful planning along with special expertise. This guide will help you create the perfect diet plan for your best friend.

Here are some common myths and misconceptions.

"Fresh foods will provide a healthy diet for my dog if I change up the ingredients from time to time."

Diets based on purely fresh ingredients can still come up short on vitamins and minerals.

"A dietary supplement can cover all the lacking nutrients."

This will not target specific deficiencies and may not be compatible with your dog's special diet.

"I'll add yogurt to his diet so he'll get enough calcium."

It's true that dogs need large amounts of calcium per day. What's not true is that adding yogurt will provide enough calcium. Feed your dog raw bones or baked and crushed eggshells. A teaspoon of these powdered eggshells equals approximately 2,200 mg of calcium carbonate.

"If I apply what I read from my human nutrition books to my dog's diet, that will be fine." This is a very common misconception, and it is also very inaccurate. The advisable ratios of food for a human diet are not appropriate for dogs.

"My dog is suffering from loose bowel movements. I'll just cut his fiber consumption to make the problem go away."

Feed your dog bland meals, or reduce his food by at least 30% for a day and see what happens. This could be a symptom of a parasitic infestation or poisoning. Consult with the veterinarian as soon as possible.

"I let my dog eat a lot of vegetables because they're the healthiest."

Some vegetables hinder the absorption of certain essential vitamins and minerals in dogs.

"Dogs don't need carbohydrates and grains. These are bad for their health."

Carbohydrates and grains are good sources of energy for your dog, and also positively benefit your dog's gastrointestinal function.

"Raw meals are healthier than cooked meals. They won't make your dog sick."

These diets are very suitable for wild dogs such as wolves, but sometimes don't work well for domesticated ones. Consult with a vet about this, research, and plan carefully. There can be harmful bacteria in raw foods if it is not handled properly.

"Raw meals are dangerous."

It is incorrect that raw diets are necessarily either too dangerous or more effective. Some vets suggest that owners feed their dogs raw meals if they are experiencing allergies or other specific illnesses. Some also suggest this diet even if the dogs are completely healthy.

"My pup and my senior share meals; they're fresh and whole foods anyway."

Puppies need two to five times the nutrient content found in adult dog food. The pup may become undernourished and the senior, particularly giant-breed dogs, may experience hyper-nutrition. New findings say puppies need more protein than seniors.

Become knowledgeable in canine nutrition before you introduce a homemade diet plan to your dog. Poor nutrition will harm your dog, no matter her age. It is best that you work with a specialist in this field, such as an animal nutritionist or a vet.

What Should Be in a Dog Diet?

Necessary Nutrients That Should Be Part of Your Dog Food

The image of a happy family often includes kids creating ruckus alongside a happy, fluffy dog. The perfect picture for a perfect household! As much as you care for your family's well-being, it is important that the dog's health is also taken care of.

We all know the importance of nutrition in our daily lives. Similarly, when feeding the cherished family pet, it's important to learn a thing or two about dog nutrition. This will help you get the right food, either packaged or homemade. A well-balanced dog food will provide a good diet for all kinds of dogs: puppies, adult dogs, pregnant dogs, or dogs with special health concerns.

An important ingredient you should look for when you buy raw dog food is that it should have plenty of meat and big, juicy, meaty bones. These give the dog plenty of protein to help provide balanced nutrition, support her immune system, and also ensure the overall health of the animal.

Contrary to common belief, a dog's diet should not be limited to meat. It is equally important that the dog is fed vitamins, minerals, and fiber. Vegetables and fruits should be given in adequate quantity to make sure that the dog gets a balanced diet. Vegetables provide the dog with essential vitamins such as A, B, C, and K. Vitamins help improve eyesight, and also take care of the other sensory organs. Vegetables also play an important role in providing fiber to the dog, helping the digestive system.

Dog food should also have adequate amounts of fruit and organs, particularly liver. While liver has vitamins, minerals and other nutrients like B12, zinc, iron, and omega-3 fatty acids, fruits give the much required vitamin C to the dog. All this put together helps the dog maintain a lean body and a correct weight. Immunity also becomes strong with such a diet.

If you prefer packaged dog food, remember that though it may be processed, it should also have the above-mentioned items in good quantity. Raw packaged food is a natural choice for most households, and it is good as long as it gives wholesome, complete nutrition to the dog. There are various kinds of packaged food available on the market and you need to do some research before you decide on a particular brand or product. Keeping the breed in mind, and understanding that kind of dog's needs will help you make a wise decision.

What Are the Protein Requirements for Dogs in Their Diet?

As a dog owner, you would want to give your dog a high quality diet. But with the many brands and kinds of dog food and the limited (and often incorrect) information circulating, choosing and judging the best dog food for your dog becomes a difficult task.

How important is protein in the diet?

Proteins are a necessary component of the diet because they are used for growth. Proteins are also essential for all bodily functions including those of the brain, heart, skin, skeleton and many others. Proteins are important as source of amino acids necessary for building hair, skin, nails, muscles, tendons, ligaments, and cartilage. Proteins are also important in the synthesis of hormones and enzymes that are necessary for body function.

Protein requirements

Protein requirements of dogs vary with age, activity level, temperament, life stage, health status, and protein quality of the diet.

Puppies require higher protein content in their diet. Puppy food should contain a minimum of 22% protein (as dry matter). Adult dogs require a minimum of 18% protein (as dry matter).

Do not feed your puppy an adult maintenance diets because, adult diets have fewer nutrients compared to puppy formulations. Growing little dogs need more.

Also, if you are afraid that a high protein diet will overload the kidneys and cause disease, then you are definitely misinformed.

Studies have shown that high protein intake DOES NOT cause skeletal abnormalities in dogs, or renal insufficiency later in life.

Protein sources

Dogs need protein with high biologic value. The biologic value of a protein relates to the number and types of essential amino acids and how easy it is to digest and metabolize the protein. The greater the biologic value of a protein, the less protein is needed in the diet to supply the essential amino acid requirements.

Meat-based proteins, particularly those from organ and skeletal meats, have higher biologic value than plant-based proteins like those from corn or cereals. Make sure to check the protein source of a particular dog food the next time you buy. Choose one that has its protein source from meat like chicken, lamb, or beef.

In choosing dog foods with chicken, make sure the ingredients lists it as "chicken meal." Chicken meal is better in this case than chicken meat or chicken parts, because meat or parts contain about 75% water, whereas most of the water has been removed from the meal. Chicken meal, therefore, contains a proportionally higher protein content.

Eggs are an excellent source of protein, and they have the highest biologic value – the highest amount of essential amino acids. Eggs also contain vitamins and minerals (vitamins A, B, E, K, biotin and sulfur). They also contain fatty acids such as omega-6 for a healthy skin and coat of hair.

Another excellent source of protein is catfish meal. Made by drying the catfish at a low temperature, catfish meal contains highly digestible protein. Plus, catfish meal is also a great source of DHA and EPA, the most important of all the omega-3 fatty acids.

What Kinds of Foods Should Be Included in My Dog's Diet, Then?

The point of you making dog food from scratch is to make sure that your dog is being fed a complete and balanced diet. Unfortunately, if you feed your dog the same meal for weeks, this would just as easily become counterproductive. If you have a puppy, remember that they are more prone to nutritional deficiencies and excesses than adult dogs.

Here are some things to know about various foods and how they affect your dog.

Vegetables and Fruits: These provide fiber that aids in your pooch's digestive health. They also contain antioxidants and many other nutrients that help in longevity and overall health. With more active and underweight dogs, potatoes, sweet potatoes, pumpkins, legumes, or beans will aid in weight control. These vegetables have a high calorie count and contain carbohydrates. However, large amounts of these are not advisable for feeding to overweight or obese dogs. Papaya, apples, melons, berries, and bananas are recommended fruits to be served to dogs. Dark colored fruits and veggies are very nutritious, but be warned – grapes can cause fatal kidney failure and should never be given to a dog.

Warning! Garlic and anything closely related to it, such as onion or chives, contains compounds which can harm a dog's red blood cells. The damage typically does not become evident until four to five days later. You may notice weakness, or an unwillingness to move, and your dog's urine can be dark red or orange in color.

Another thing to avoid is hops. Raw or cooked hops are to be avoided as they can poison your dog. If your dog has ingested hops, he will experience a very high body temperature which can lead to multiple organ failures.

Animal Products and Meat: At least half of the diet you will prepare for your dog must be rich in proteins. However, raw meat can also be high in fat, which can cause obesity.

If your dog is overweight, he must get more exercise. Take him on long walks, or running with you. Also, make sure to use lean meat in his meals. Lean meat contains 10% fat. If you are preparing chicken, always slice off the excess fat and remove the skin. It is advisable to feed him dark poultry meat if your dog is on a low-fat diet.

Fish is very rich in vitamin D, which helps in the absorption of calcium, so it is very important. Canned sardines which are soaked in water (not oil), jack mackerel, and pink salmon are highly recommended. If you choose to buy raw fish, never buy pacific salmon, trout, or other related fish. Debone them before cooking. Only feed your dogs a ratio one pound of fish per pound of other animal meat. Feed them only a small amount of fish daily, or a larger amount once or twice every week.

Also, **chocolate should not be given to your dog, as it contains methylxanthines which can cause vomiting, restlessness, and abdominal pain.** The level of methylxanthines varies, but the darker the chocolate is, the more methyxanthines it contains. Lastly, you have to make sure to check the labels of any food you give to your dog. Any product which contains xylitol must not be eaten by dogs, as xylitol can affect your dog's sugar level, and too much can lead to seizures or fatal liver failure.

Our dogs are part of our families, and like family, we would always want to feed them the most delicious and nutritious food there is. We just have to make sure that these meals provide a complete and balanced diet and are cooked in appropriate proportions. These guidelines will help you ensure that your best friend gets the best nutrition you can provide.

What Human Foods Are Safe for Your Dog?

When your sweet old golden retriever is looking up at you with those big eyes while you're eating, it's difficult to resist the urge to give her the remainder of what's left on your plate. However, any responsible dog owner knows that certain foods just aren't good for dogs. In fact, some foods can make her very ill.

So what foods can you feed to your dog? There are some human foods that are actually good for her. While her own food should make up the majority of her dietary intake, the following foods are okay to give her in moderation:

• **Salmon**. The heart-healthy fat in salmon is loaded with omega-3s and is great for her coat and skin. Raw salmon should never be fed to dogs (as it can carry parasites) but salmon oil and cooked salmon are just fine.

• **Sweet potatoes**. Sweet potatoes contain fiber, beta carotene, vitamin B6, and vitamin C. Dogs love them as a treat because they're sweet, and you can feel good about letting your dog have some, because they are loaded with nutrients.

• **Apples**. Apples have loads of fiber and other vitamins and are another great treat for your dog. Do not let her eat the seeds as they contain arsenic. (Of course she would have to eat quite a few to harm her, but it's not a good habit to get into.)

• **Beans**. Surprisingly, dogs really like beans. Some prefer garbanzos and others like black beans. Although canned is fine, if you feel like buying a bag of dried beans, soaking and then cooking them according to the directions, your dog will get more of the benefits without all the salt. If you're using canned beans, just make sure to drain them and rinse them thoroughly. Dogs don't need all that salt in their diets.

- **Brewer's Yeast.** If your dog is a picky eater, sometimes this will help. Brewer's yeast is found in health food stores and can be sprinkled on your dog's food to stimulate her appetite. Brewer's yeast has loads of B vitamins.

- **Most vegetables.** The thing with vegetables is that while it's great for your dog to have the fiber, her digestive tract is significantly shorter than yours. Therefore, you should steam her veggies for at least three minutes, cool them off and then put them in the blender for her. A purée is the best way to help her absorb the nutrients.

- **Raw bones.** If you've been considering a raw diet for your dog, you're not alone. Raw meat and bones are very nutritious for your dog. Proponents of the raw diet argue that it mimics what she would eat if she were in the wild, which includes many raw bones. They do have plenty of calcium, which helps build strong teeth and bones. However, veterinarians explain that they do see cases where even raw bones can become lodged in a dog's throat or digestive system, so caution is recommended. If you're in doubt, purchase ground raw bones, or try giving larger, raw meaty bones to your dog frozen, so they need to eat them more slowly. Some suggest that this can help reduce the risk of choking. Don't use small bones like chicken.

You will know when you have fed your dog something that doesn't agree with her. Symptoms can range from weakness and diarrhea to paralysis. Such symptoms require an immediate visit to the vet.

What Human Foods Are NOT Safe for Your Dog?

Most commercial dog foods are full of allergens, toxins, and carcinogens, and the ingredients are a poor source of nutrition; therefore, making your own dog food remains the surest way to know what goes into your dog's diet. The starting point is knowing how! Switching your dog's diet from commercial dog food to healthy, homemade dog food will be of great benefit to the overall health of your beloved pet. Making your own dog food using the right ingredients will boost the health of your dog, support his immune system, and help reduce the possibility of cancer as a result of poor food ingredients. When making your dog food the following ingredients should be avoided:

Avocadoes. Avocadoes have a substance in them that is toxic to dogs, called persin. Even the leaves, seeds, and bark of the plant are toxic so you must keep your dog away from any avocadoes that you grow in your yard – and keep her out of any compost too.

• **Onions and garlic**. These destroy dogs' red blood cells and can cause anemia in larger doses! The same goes for garlic. Don't feed your dog anything with onion or garlic in the ingredients.

• **Grapes**. Some people feed grapes or their dehydrated version, raisins, to their dogs but it is not a good idea. Even small amounts of grapes can make your dog sick and she may start vomiting and become lethargic. This is a sign of kidney failure. If you keep a fruit bowl on your table full of grapes, make sure that your dog cannot reach it.

• **Macadamia Nuts**. Macadamia nuts are toxic to your dog, so keep them far away from her. It does not take very many nuts to make her extremely ill, especially if they are mixed with chocolate.

• **Candy**. The rapid spike and crash in blood sugar that candy causes is not good for humans – but it is devastating to a dog. It can cause vomiting, seizures, and if given often, eventual liver failure.

• **Chocolate**. By now it's pretty well documented that chocolate is bad for dogs. It can cause seizures and even kill them.

• **Cooked bones**. Cooking bones changes the chemical composition, which can cause splintering and harm to your dog's mouth and digestive system, such as punctures that require surgery to correct. It's never a good idea to give dogs cooked bones.

• **Ham and bacon.** These highly processed meats are salty and contain chemicals, and they are often excessively high in fat. They should be used in moderation.

• **Tomatoes.** Tomatoes are too acidic for your dog.

A Note about Grass

A bushy green lawn, with blades of tall green grass can be a fabulous smorgasbord for your dog! As with any food buffet, the temptation to linger until you've eaten too much happens with dogs too. Canines can enjoy an omnivorous diet, meaning they enjoy vegetation in addition to meat products – so eating grass is normal, if done in moderation.

However, if your dog binges on grass, this is a sign of an upset stomach. Your dog feels the need to remove the discomfort of gas, constipation, or diarrhea, and eating grass acts as a stimulant to encourage vomiting. By emptying the stomach your dog is trying to feel better. That's right! Your dog is smart, and know when it's time to improve her digestion. Such instinctive behavior may also help to fulfill a nutritional need. So, before you become annoyed or take drastic steps to prevent your dog's behavior of eating grass, re-evaluate the situation, and allow your dog to provide self-care. More than likely your dog is purposefully adding some roughage, and using it as an antidote for spoiled food. In addition, it is comforting to know that grass has digestive enzymes.

However, there is an important caution to mention about dogs eating grass. Be careful that the grass your dog is eating has not been sprayed or treated with pesticides or lawn fertilizers.

It's also possible that your dog is eating grass because she needs more fiber in her diet. There are ways you can help. For instance, try substituting cooked rice and chicken for part of her food, or adding boiled potato chunks. Keep this up until your dog is feeling better.

If your dog is suffering from constipation, remember exercise is important. Take her out for walks, and let her run, jump and play. Also, ensure she is getting plenty of water.

Treats and Supplements

Treats are an invaluable tool for training your dog, but keep in mind they should make up 5% or less of your dog's daily intake of food. The good news is, if you choose treats carefully, they can contribute important nutrients to your dog's diet.

What are the benefits of velvet antler dog treats for your dog's health?

Aside from being delicious chews for dogs, velvet antler dog treats are also very healthy for dogs suffering from joint inflammation. Usually, they are made from either deer or elk antlers.

Various deer grow antlers which regenerate each year, in spring. At first, after regeneration happens, the new pair is a soft cartilage, which mineralizes as time passes. In late summer, the antlers are transformed into bones. A soft fur known as velvet develops on the surface of the antlers as they grow. The role of the velvet is to provide protection, and it is rubbed off by the deer once the antlers are fully grown, as it is no longer needed. The shed layer is what is used for velvet antler dog treats.

There are various healthy minerals that can be found in deer antlers, such as calcium, phosphorous and zinc, as well as chondroitin sulfate, omega-3 and -6, and glycosaminoglycans. These substances positively affect joint function, as they help reduce inflammation and relieve pain. Fluids are attracted by the substances contained in these antlers, which offer support to the cartilage. The role of the fluid is to absorb shocks and also to provide nutrients, so the cartilage does not become fragile, malnourished and dried – an important role in preventing arthritis and reducing pain and swelling caused by joint inflammation. That is why a dog's joint health can benefit from the use of velvet antler treats.

These treats are beneficial for your dog's oral health as well, however, as they keep the teeth healthy and clean. Also, antler treats are good for dogs who need to recover after having surgery or having suffered injuries. Blood circulation, the immune system, and the level of energy your dog has are also positively influenced by antler supplements.

It should be said that if you give your dog antler chews, you should be careful and make sure the dog does not choke on the treat. Be sure to supervise the dog, and take smaller, soggy, or sharp pieces away. Velvet antler treats can be found as chews but also as chips or powder.

If your dog suffers from joint pain, you will surely want to offer it proper treatment, exercise, and a diet that is appropriate for its health condition. **Velvet antler dog treats have a positive impact on dog joints and overall health**, and are a good option for helping your pet feel better.

A Few Healthy Treats You Can You Make For Your Dog

Interested in dog treats? Well, if you're a dog person, you not only enjoy the company of your dog, but you are also preoccupied with his health and happiness. You'll take him for walks, buy him toys, care for his fur and choose the best food possible for his needs. In the following section, we will discuss some great treats for dogs.

There are excellent dog treats to be found on the market and there are others that you yourself can prepare. In specialized stores, you will usually find treats that are made with all natural ingredients, which is very important. For example, you can find products that contain rice, ground apples, berries, carrots, or parsley, along with other ingredients that have been chosen to help build strong cartilage and lubricate the joints. Such products are usually developed keeping in mind that food – even treats – impacts the fur and stomach health. Other natural dog treats place a bigger importance on the meat percentage that is contained in the product. They often contain dried beef liver, for example, sometimes along with active ingredients that are aimed at reducing aches in aging joints. The best dog treats will make your dog energetic and lively.

If you would like to alternate using market products with preparing healthy treats for your dog at home, here are two recipes we suggest:

Fruity Oat Treats

Ingredients
2 cups rolled oats, divided

3 dates

1 banana, mashed

1 teaspoon apple cider vinegar

2 tablespoons organic flaxseed oil

1 teaspoon spirulina

1 teaspoon honey

Directions
In a blender or food processor, combine one cup of oats, the dates, the banana and the vinegar. Transfer the mixture to a mixing bowl, and add the remaining oats, flaxseed oil, spirulina, and honey. Mix well, and then put it into a shallow dish and flatten it down. Refrigerate for approximately 30 minutes. Cut it into rectangles to make biscuit-like treats.

This treat should be helpful, especially if your dog suffers from any skin problems.

Quick and Easy Peanut Butter Treats

Ingredients
¼ cup sunflower seeds

2 cups flour

½ cup apples, chopped

¼ cup mixed vegetables, such as carrots and peas

¼ cup oats, ground to a powder

1 cup peanut butter

1 cup rolled oats

1 cup molasses

Directions

Combine all the ingredients EXCEPT the molasses in a large bowl. Mix well. Add the molasses and work it in until a stiff dough is formed. If necessary, additional oats can be added for stiffer dough. Roll out the dough to about ½-inch thick, and cut it into shapes. Arrange the shapes in a dehydrator, or dehydrate them in the oven at 150°F for around four hours. It is important that these treats are dry.

This is a usually a popular treat for horses, but it is enjoyed by dogs and cats also.

There are numerous dog treats you can find in pet stores, and others you can prepare yourself at home, so take your time and find the treat that best serves your dog's needs.

Glucosamine and Chondroitin for Dogs

Dogs of any age can benefit greatly by incorporating glucosamine in their diets. Glucosamine aids in reducing inflammation, pain, and swelling in the joints of dogs, as it increases the flexibility in their joints. If we pay close attention to the health of our dog's joints, bones, eyes, and coat and providing appropriate grooming, food and supplements, our canine companion can enjoy the happy, healthy, and active life she deserves. When added to her diet, glucosamine helps improve your dog's mobility by reducing inflammation and swelling in their joints and extends her active years and improves her quality of life.

Commonly used as a dietary supplement, glucosamine is an amino sugar that is derived from the shells of lobsters, shrimp, and crabs. Other less common sources where glucosamine can be found include wheat, fermented corn, and some varieties of mushrooms. Glucosamine appears to provide anti-inflammatory benefits as it stimulates the cells that make cartilage. When cartilage is replenished, the joints that surround it become more lubricated and padded, which in turn reduces swelling and painful inflammation.

Chondroitin is a vital element in cartilage that helps resist compression. Used commonly in the treatment of osteoarthritis, this valuable compound is composed of various sugars that are typically attached to proteins which assist in the restoration and building of cartilage. This is an invaluable tool as well in the battle against joint discomfort and pain in canines.

Occasionally used to treat inflammation, MSM, or Methylsulfonylmethane, is an organic compound. While the effects and benefits of MSM are inadequately documented and still misunderstood, many people swear that by adding MSM to dietary supplements the pain and inflammation of arthritis is greatly reduced. Although MSM is thought to be harmless, its benefits have not been scientifically corroborated and therefore consumers are urged to not rely on MSM solely for joint treatment therapy.

Experts concur that the strong anti-inflammatory results of glucosamine, when combined with the cartilage repairing and restoring effects of chondroitin, offer efficient and effective pain relief while supporting joint health. This effective, double pronged method can be safely administered in one easy tablet. When given consistently over a period of several weeks, studies have shown that dogs given both chondroitin and glucosamine have better overall mobility.

Obtaining glucosamine and chondroitin for dogs is simple. Talk with your veterinarian for their recommendation and then follow the provided dosage guidelines. Glucosamine and chondroitin for dogs can be found in liquid, tablet, or pill forms. This offers variety in methods of administering and lets you to choose the best approach for your dog. Glucosamine and chondroitin for dogs is a very simple way to help your companion and best friend be healthy, active, pain free, and happy for as long as possible. Glucosamine and chondroitin for dogs also gives you assurance and the peace of mind that you are doing your part in protecting the health of your beloved dog. Do not delay or wait until the pain of aging joints and arthritis slows down your dog. Begin supplementing her diet with chondroitin for dogs or perhaps the combination supplement of both glucosamine and chondroitin so you and your dog can enjoy a long, happy, and active life together.

Through the Ages: Puppies and Older Dogs

If you are a new dog owner, taking care of your dog might seem daunting to you. It is understandable, though, that you would want the best for your dog, and starting to feed him home-cooked meals at a really young age can be very challenging. But do not fret and do not be afraid – the following are basic rules to help even a new dog owner provide the best nutrition for a puppy without having to worry about it too much.

Feeding Your Puppy

The First Six to Eight weeks
It is best to let the mother nurse her puppies during this stage. Let the puppies stay with the mother to get the best nutrition and to help them create the antibodies that they need to combat common diseases. The only time it is okay for them to be separated is when the mother contracts certain diseases such as mastitis, which is a bacterial infection of one or more of the lactating glands in the breasts. Eclampsia can also occur; a life-threatening drop in blood calcium which usually manifests during the time the mother is producing the most milk, commonly when the puppies are from one to five weeks. In these scenarios, you can use milk replacers or bottles which can be easily found in pet stores.

Transitioning to Solid Food
This should be done over the course of two to three weeks. Use commercial foods at this time, and make sure to buy "puppy"

foods, which contain more nutritional content than regular dog food. This supports the puppies' needs while they are growing and gaining strength.

Dog foods that are labeled "for all life stages" would be fine for a puppy as well. The best, however, are those made with a high quality, all-natural ingredients. These can be used as gruel when weaning your puppies to solid food.

Once you have selected your preferred puppy food, moisten it with warm water or milk, and wait until it is soft and mushy, like oatmeal. Place it in a shallow pan and offer it to the pups three or four times a day. Gradually reduce the amount of water or milk over the next four weeks or so, until the pups are only eating the dried kibble. They should be able to eat solid food around by the eighth week.

Feeding Frequency

Puppies should be fed three to four times a day. It is advisable to give them more frequent and smaller meals so it's easier on their digestion, and to avoid erratic energy levels. At around six months it would be fine to feed them only twice a day for convenience, but this still depends on the needs of certain breeds. Don't let them stay on puppy food too long, since this can cause obesity and orthopedic issues due to its high nutrition content. You can judge the needed amount by how much puppy food is left when you feed them, or if your puppies are showing unusual weight gain.

Keep in mind that these are just general rules for feeding puppies. Ideally, you should research more about your dog's specific breed so you can give them the most suited diet and the best nutrition.

Your Senior Dog

As the years have progressed, the greater the degree of technological advancements available. This is not only in the technology and gadgets industry, but also within medical industries, including veterinary science. Changes in medicine and nutrition have prolonged the life of different animals; however, it is still inevitable that your pet will age, and with age comes various health problems. This section will provide information on how to provide an older dog with the most appropriate geriatric care and nutrition.

The Signs of Aging

The first signs of aging among dogs are deterioration in optimal physical and psychological abilities. Even if the dog does not present with external signs of aging, one will notice that senior canines have a longer recovery time from any ailments. Furthermore, the dog is no longer able to respond as quickly to different stimuli. This is often due to less effective cognitive functioning and the presence of different physical illnesses.

The most common illness that a senior dog will experience is arthritis. Arthritis will affect the dog's movement, and contribute to a greater susceptibility to falls and stumbling. Furthermore, a dog with arthritis will find it difficult to walk and will move less, overall. If the dog is showing signs of arthritis, check with your vet about joint supplements (such as glucosamine and chondroitin, as described in this book, or the velvet antler treats) and painkillers. This medication can provide relief for the dog and will help alleviate the pain. It is also recommended that dogs with arthritis rest in warmer areas, as cold air can increase joint pain.

Another common affliction among older dogs is their inability to control their bladder and bowel movements. Symptoms of this will be bed wetting and an increased need to 'go out.'

To determine whether or not your senior dog is displaying age-related medical ailments, it is recommended that the dog has regular veterinary examinations. General geriatric examinations should be completed a minimum of twice per year and include a series of blood tests. The results will help diagnose any conditions and your veterinarian can assist in finding treatments.

As mentioned above, the most commons sign of aging within dogs is a reduction in movement and impaired responses to stimuli. One method to prevent these symptoms is to keep the dog active. Contrary to popular belief, senior dogs are as able as younger dogs to engage in highly stimulated activities – that is, they usually still want to play, and the more they do, the healthier they will be.

A final tip to mention is the regulation of the senior dog's diet. Studies have shown that senior dogs who continue to eat a regular diet are at higher risk of obesity. Specially formulated food products have been created as appropriate means of changing the dog's diet regime. If you are preparing your dog's food yourself, you will want to gradually reduce the amount you are feeding.

Canine Diet - The Golden Years

Dog owners everywhere have been following the news very closely over the past few years. Contaminated pet food has been in the headlines many times, even describing incidents of food contamination that proved fatal to some dogs, particularly older pets whose immune systems couldn't stand up to that kind of assault. It makes sense when dealing with a largely unregulated industry that many owners are evaluating how they feed their older dogs. These issues, atop the ordinary concerns over how and what to feed an aging canine, can be difficult to address.

As dogs get older their digestive systems and bowels can become weaker and more sensitive than when they were in their prime. The doggy treats they loved when they were younger can evolve into something to be avoided at all costs. Gastric distress can manifest as simple gas, or in more serious ways through vomiting and diarrhea. All these, in addition to other more blatant health issues such as loss of eyesight and canine arthritis, need to be addressed when considering the ins and outs of feeding an older dog. Before addressing the issue, let's first look at the best method to use regarding frequency and volume.

Volume and Frequency

Older dogs tend to become less active, preferring a more sedentary lifestyle than when they were in their peak years. Consequently, their caloric needs drop significantly, often as much as 20-30%. Although the calories and nutritional requirements differ greatly from breed to breed, any owner should know that when their pet starts to slow down, their feed should drop accordingly. Additionally, as with humans, changes made to the volume of the animal's daily intake should be gradual – older animals react even less well to large scale change than we humans do.

In respect to the frequency of feeding, it's much better for dogs – especially older dogs – to eat smaller meals spread over the course of the day. As activity drops, large meals can have an extreme and adverse effect on old dogs; too much food for an aging stomach to process can cause indigestion. Worse, even if it doesn't cause immediate problems, the excess calories from that meal are much more likely to be stored as fat, shaving years from the dog's lifespan.

The best practice for frequency is to feed two to three meals a day, depending on how active the animal is on a daily basis – more activity means more leeway for fewer feedings. The more inactive a dog is, the more crucial it becomes that he eat his meals spread out over the course of the day.

Dogs with Special Medical Conditions

Cancer

The incidence of cancer both in people and dogs has increased in the past years, while at the same time retaining an aura of mystery as medical science continues the search for its underlying cause. However, the treatment of cancer in dogs and man has experienced some significant progress. The goals of cancer treatment in dogs are mainly stymieing the spread of the cancerous cells, and where possible, getting rid of the cancerous tissues in order to restore the dog back to complete health.

As a dog owner you should be aware of the signs of cancer in dogs so that you are able to respond quickly. If you notice a lump or a bump on your dog, or a foul odor emanating from the ears, mouth, or any other part of the dog's body, take him to be checked.

There are quite a few treatment options available for dogs suffering from cancer; many with a proven record of success – particularly if the cancer is detected in the early stages. The veterinarian may do a biopsy, and send the results to a pathology lab, where the type of tumor can be identified. Then the vet will assess the outlook for your pet, and together you can establish a course of action.

If the cancerous cells have not yet spread, which is often the case when it is detected in the early stages, then surgery is the best option to remove the localized cancerous tissues, and there is a very high probability of success. Beyond that point, other treatment options such as radiation or chemotherapy will have to be used.

Feeding Your Dog after a Cancer Diagnosis

It is true that there have been many medical advancements in the fight against cancer in recent years, benefitting both humans and our beloved pets. However, the fight is far from over. Here are some interesting points about cancer in dogs:

- About 50% of disease-related deaths in dogs is caused by cancer, and the disease takes 25% of dogs overall. It is the foremost natural cause of death in older dogs.
- Dogs get afflicted with cancer at about the same rate as humans.
- Dogs can get cancer in any part of their body, just like human beings, and 25% will develop some kind of tumor during their lifetime.
- Just as with human beings, the cause of cancer in dogs is largely unknown.
- Obesity in dogs increases the risk of cancer.

If your dog has been diagnosed with cancer, it is important that special attention be paid to his diet. With or without other treatment, his immune system need to be supported so it can help in the fight against the cancer cells. And depending on the cancer therapy that your dog is undergoing, this may put an additional burden on his system. It is very important that he grows new tissues during therapy and the most effective way to help your dog's body grow the new tissues is by feeding him on the right diet. If a dog has cancer and does not get enough nutrients, his body will draw the needed nutrients from other parts of his body in order to meet the need. This could result in his muscles weakening, and potential difficulties with the liver of kidneys.

Part of feeding your dog with cancer on the right diet involves knowing the foods that should be kept away from him and one such food is grains. Some of the most essential foods for dogs with cancer are:

- Animal protein such as eggs, canned sardines, chicken, ground turkey and cheese.
- Food with high fat content.
- Fish oil, which contains Omega 3, 6 and 9 which helps in the fight against cancer.

Liver Disease

Liver disease in dogs is a common disorder that is known to predominately affect older dogs, and there are many different causes. Statistics show that liver disease accounts for one-fifth of non-accidental deaths of dogs. The liver is a very important organ in dogs – just as in human beings – and it performs several functions, such as the storage of energy and nutrients, detoxification of the body, fighting diseases, and a lot more. Therefore if the liver becomes diseased and is no longer able to perform its functions, then the dog will soon begin to suffer. The prognosis of a diseased liver hinges on early detection and prompt treatment.

Liver disease in dogs can be caused by chronic hepatitis, injury to the abdomen, heart disease, anemia, virus, bacteria, fungus, and inflammation of the pancreas. Trauma, like being struck by a car or a severe heat stroke can also result in a diseased liver, and some drugs that are used in treating other medical conditions (like worming medications) may also be factors. Some dogs are born with a liver abnormality that can develop into the disease.

A very common symptom of liver disease in dogs is lethargy and depression, and you may also notice a distended stomach as a result of an enlarged liver. Some other symptoms to be on the lookout for include vomiting, weight loss, diarrhea, urination, excessive drinking, and a drop in appetite. When the disease gets to an advanced stage without treatment, usually because of late detection, then you may observe the yellowing of his gums, the whites of his eyes, and his skin. Liver disease in dogs can easily go undetected, and in some cases can be mistaken for other health related issues. If you notice any of the possible symptoms in your dog, promptly visit the vet and talk about your observations.

The prognosis and the treatment of a diseased liver depends on the cause of the disease. For instance, if it is caused by trauma then hospitalization may be all that is needed for complete recovery, whereas if the cause is due to bacteria, virus, or a fungal infection, then antibiotics will have to be administered. In most cases dietary changes will be necessary; this may involve nothing more than adjusting the quantities of vitamins, minerals, proteins, fats, and carbohydrates that you give to your beloved pet.

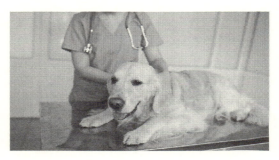

Dogs with Allergies and Sensitivities

Finding the Best Food for your Dog with Allergies

A dog suffering from allergies is often a distressing sight. These poor dogs often scratch themselves raw or suffer from chronic and painful ear infections. Often, we find that an ingredient in the food is a culprit. The number of food allergy cases has continually risen through the years – clinical cases show that more than 10% of all dog allergies have been linked to food. Aside from plant proteins, there are dogs which can be hypersensitive to beef, chicken, lamb, egg, pork, fish, and dairy products. Many dog owners have become increasingly concerned about giving only the best food to their dogs for this reason.

Most food allergies are triggered by specific types of proteins present in dog food formulations. If you take time to closely examine the ingredients of commercial dog food, you will find that the protein component comes from not only meat but also from grains and vegetables. By nature, dogs are carnivores – thus, they are mainly meat-eaters. Incorporating grains and vegetables in their diet may potentially upset the metabolic processes of your dog's body and can eventually lead to adverse reactions.

Most cases of food allergies in dogs are genetic in nature. This genetic predisposition increases their sensitivity to developing allergies from any food that they take in.

When your dog has been suffering from chronic health problems such as itching, ear infections, or gastrointestinal problems, your vet may suspect a food allergy. This is especially true when your dog's problems have failed to respond positively to specific medications.

If you suspect that your dog is suffering from food allergies, the best thing you can do is conduct an "elimination diet and challenge." This involves removing all the usual food that has been a part of your dog's daily diet, and giving him food that contains ingredients he has never had before.

Once the allergen has been removed from your dog's diet, positive changes are easily noticeable within a short period of time. You can now start to slowly reintroduce the old foods to determine which dog food or feed ingredient caused your dog's allergy problems in the first place. By doing so, you will be able to identify the food your dog is allergic to and buy (or make) only dog foods that do not contain the ingredient.

Whatever way you choose to address your dog's food allergy problems, you should remember that the best dog foods for allergies do not incorporate ingredients which have been identified as potential allergens. As you can see, you may have a hard time looking for the best commercial dog food for your dog, since most of them contain two or more of these identified potential allergens.

Your best bet would be to select or make dog food that contains only two or three protein sources. In this way, if your dog will develop hypersensitive reactions to its food, you can easily pinpoint the allergen thereby easily correcting the problem.

Food allergies in dogs can often be challenging and difficult to deal with. By being an attentive dog owner and selecting only the best dog food for allergies, you will be able to free and protect your dog from food allergies.

Gluten Free Dog Food

Sometimes, if a dog has ongoing health problems, gluten may be the issue. Gluten has been seen to contribute to canine health problems such as joint pain, allergies, ear infections, canine diabetes, and even celiac disease. The good news is, the solution might be as simple as switching to gluten free food.

Commercial dog foods often do contain foods that are high in gluten. In 2007, hundreds of pets died or got sick when wheat gluten in their food was tainted, and this led many pet owners to begin to question what is actually in their pets' food. We also began to realize how much wheat and corn these foods contain, as inexpensive filler.

What can you do?
Changing your dog's food too rapidly can sometimes lead to stomach upset, so proceed slowly. It's best to substitute a quarter of the food at a time, gradually increasing the ratio of gluten free food until wheat, corn, rye, barley, and other sources of gluten are fully eliminated.

If your dog is sensitive to gluten, use the recipes in this book to ensure that his diet is ok for him. For recipes that contain flour, you can experiment with substituting gluten free flour blends, available at grocery and bulk food stores. You can even make them yourself, using rice flour, potato or tapioca starch, arrowroot flour, and many others. Talk to your veterinarian to make sure you are meeting all your dog's nutritional needs.

If your dog still has symptoms, you may want to try eliminating dairy, as well, again, under the guidance of your dog's vet.

Recipes for Growing Puppies

Now that you know the importance of good nutrition and how to make sure it's in your dog's diet, it's time for you to begin to prepare your dog's meals personally! Aside from being good for your dog, it may also be more budget-friendly as well.

Go ahead and check out these nutritious recipes.

Puppy Stew
Makes about 32 cups

Ingredients
3 pounds boneless chicken (skin on, but you can remove the skin if you feel that's too rich for the dog)

6 large sweet potatoes (peeled and diced)

6 large carrots (peeled and chopped)

2 cups barley or rice

56 ounces tomatoes (juice included)

½ cup oil (choose from fish, olive, or safflower)

Medium pack lima beans or frozen peas

3 tablespoons fresh oregano or parsley

1 teaspoon salt water (use iodized)

Directions

Place all the ingredients in a 3-gallon pot. Add more than enough water to cover all the ingredients. Bring it to boil. Lower the heat and simmer, covered.

Cook for about 2 hours, until all the ingredients are soft and the liquid decreases. Stir occasionally. If the mixture becomes a bit dry, add more water.

Turn off the heat and divide the stew into containers.

Delicious Brunch for Pups

Makes about 8 cups

Ingredients

2 cups plain yogurt

2 tablespoons safflower oil

1 piece apple or pear (cored and chopped)

1 banana (peeled and mashed)

2 cups cottage cheese

1 cup ripe mango (peeled and mashed)

Directions

Combine all the ingredients in a large bowl. Mix well, and refrigerate. (Don't freeze.)

Once the mixture is cold, serve it to your puppy.

Home-made Basic Puppy Food

Makes about 10 cups

Ingredients

½ cup zucchini (chopped)

½ cup apples (cored and seeded)

½ cup carrots (chopped)

1 small can sardines

¼ cup olive oil

2 ½ cups brown rice (uncooked)

2 pounds boneless skinless chicken, diced

7 cups clean water

Directions

Place all the ingredients in a slow cooker. Cook on high for 6 to 7 hours.

Once the rice is thoroughly cooked, you can set the mixture aside to cool.

You can replace the veggies with others like peas, green beans, sweet potatoes, or plum. Lamb or beef can also be used in place of chicken.

A Chicky (or Fishy) Affair

Makes about 80 pieces

Ingredients

2 cups sweet potatoes (peeled, cooked, and mashed)

1 cup low sodium chicken or beef broth

4 cups whole wheat flour

1 (5.5 ounce) can chicken or salmon (boned and skinned, drain well)

¼ cup oil (you can use fish, olive, or safflower oil)

1 teaspoon iodized salt

4 tablespoons dried parsley

Directions

In a large mixing bowl, combine all the ingredients until a paste is formed.

Roll out the mixture on a lightly-floured cutting board, to a ¼-inch thickness. Cut it into around 80 pieces.

Place the pieces on a baking sheet lined with parchment paper.

Preheat the oven to 300°F and bake the pieces for about 45 minutes on the center rack.

Remove the cooked pieces and let them stand for about 3-4 hours, or overnight, to dry. Store in an airtight container.

Chicken Chews

Ingredients
2-4 boneless, skinless chicken breasts

Directions
Preheat the oven to 200°F.

Remove any extra fat from the chicken, and slice it in about ⅛-inch strips.

Place the strips on the baking tray and bake for about 2 hours.

To check whether the chicken is ready, make sure that the texture is hard and dry, not chewy or soft.

Remove the tray from the oven once the proper consistency is achieved. Cool, and set aside.

Store in an airtight container and place it in a refrigerator. This will last for about a week or two. You can also use sweet potatoes to replace the chicken if you want a vegetarian snack.

Chicken with Spinach Puppy food

Ingredients

1 ½ cups dry brown rice (cooked per package directions)

1 tablespoon olive oil

4 pounds ground chicken

1 large yam, or 2 small ones

1 ½ chicken broth

4-5 cups fresh spinach

Directions

Wash the yam and pierce it using a fork. Cook it in the microwave for about 7 minutes on high, until it becomes tender.

Once the yam is cooked, set it aside and let it cool. Cut it into small cubes.

Using a large pot, heat the oil and cook the chicken until it becomes brown.

Remove the pot from the heat. Add the yams, tomato sauce, spinach, and cooked rice. Mix well. Use an immersion blender and continue mixing. The texture should look like dog food and there should be no big chunks. Let it cool for around an hour. Put it in the refrigerator to further set the mixture.

Meanwhile, line two large baking trays with parchment paper. Take the mixture out of the refrigerator and scoop out a serving amount and place it on the baking tray.

Put the tray in the freezer until the food becomes frozen. This food will last for about a month.

Barking Puppy Breakfast

Ingredients

2 eggs

2 slices bacon

3 slices bread, toasted

¼ cup cheese, grated

Directions

Scramble and cook the eggs, and fry the bacon.

Place the food in a bowl and sprinkle some cheese on top. Serve.

Puppy Meatloaf

Ingredients

¾ cup veggies (assorted, according to your preference)

1 ½ cups oatmeal

2 pounds lean ground beef

2 eggs

½ cup cottage cheese

Flax seeds (ground)

Directions

Preheat the oven to 350°F.

Combine all the ingredients and press the mixture into a well-greased baking or meatloaf pan. Bake for 20 to 30 minutes. (You can serve this medium rare.) Cut into small pieces. Serve.

Almond and Banana Puppy Treats

Ingredients

⅓ of a banana

¾ cup almond butter (unsalted)

1 egg

1 teaspoon cinnamon (ground)

Directions

Preheat the oven to 350°F. Line a baking pan with parchment paper.

Mash the banana with a fork, and then add the rest of the ingredients. Mix well. The batter should be gooey and thick.

Spoon dollops of the mixture onto the baking pan. Bake for around 5 minutes, and then flip the pieces over. Bake once again for another 5 minutes.

Remove from the oven. Let them cool, then serve.

Puppy Tex-Mex

Ingredients

4 chicken breasts (sliced)

1 cup black beans (canned, drained)

1 cup kidney beans (canned, drained)

½ cup tomato paste

1 cup carrots (diced)

4 cups chicken broth

Directions

Cook the chicken in a medium-sized, non-stick skillet over medium heat.

Add the beans, tomato paste, carrots, and broth, and cook for around 20 minutes on medium heat. Let cool, then serve.

Chicken Apple Pup Pops

Ingredients
1 apple (diced)

½ cup unsalted chicken broth

Rawhide pork strips

Directions
Place the apple pieces in 2 paper drinking cups. Fill it halfway with the chicken broth.

Place some rawhide pork sticks in the center then freeze it for around 3 hours.

Once the mixture is already frozen, peel off the paper cups and serve.

Spinach Salmon Puppy Chow

Ingredients
2 tablespoons olive oil

1 (16 ounce) package spinach (frozen; thawed)

1 (15 ounce) can boneless salmon

2 eggs

Directions
Heat the oil in the pan on low to medium heat. Cook the spinach with the salmon until it is heated through.

Meanwhile, whisk the eggs, then pour them on the pan with the mixture. Stir well until eggs are cooked. Let it cool, then serve.

Mini Omelets

Ingredients
2 eggs

1 piece smoked salmon (sliced thinly)

1 green pepper (diced)

Directions
Lightly grease a ramekin using a small amount of olive oil. Crack the eggs into the ramekin.

Add the salmon and the green pepper. Mix lightly using a fork until it is combined well.

Bake at 350°F for 12 minutes, or until the top is slightly browned. Cool and serve.

Crunchy Apple Pupcakes

Ingredients

¼ cup unsweetened applesauce

2 tablespoons honey

2 ¾ cups water

1 medium egg

⅛ tablespoon of vanilla extract

4 cups whole wheat flour

1 tablespoon baking powder

1 cup apple chips (dried and unsweetened)

Directions

Preheat the oven to 350°F. Grease a muffin pan.

Mix the applesauce, honey, water, egg, and vanilla extract in a medium-sized bowl. Combine well.

Add the rest of the ingredients and lightly mix until well combined.

Spoon the mixture into the muffin cups, and bake for about 1 hour Let them cool, then serve.

Plain Mash Doggie Food

Ingredients
2 boneless skinless chicken breasts

1 cup of white rice (cooked)

½ cup warm water, more if needed

Directions
Boil the chicken, and shred it with two forks.

Mix the shredded chicken with the cooked rice, and add the warm water. Mash together, and serve.

Sweet Mix and Mash

Ingredients
¼ cup canned pumpkin (pureed)

2 tablespoons yogurt

Directions
Mix all the ingredients in a bowl and serve. Make sure that the puree is pumpkin and not the pie filling. It should include only pumpkin.

Scooby Dooby Stew

Ingredients

1 cup brown rice

2 large chicken breasts

2 ½ cups water

2 cups sweet potato, cubed

2 pounds mixed veggies (frozen)

Directions

Combine all the ingredients in a slow cooker. Make sure the chicken is completely covered with the veggies.

Cook on high for 5 hours on high, or 8 hours on low.

Remove the chicken from the cooker and shred it, then mix it back in. Serve.

Rice Porridge

Ingredients

12 cups water

2 cups rice

2 tablespoons vegetable oil

2 scallions (chopped finely)

2 cups bok choy (you may also use Swiss chard)

1 teaspoon ginger (grated)

1 tablespoon tamari sauce

1 tablespoon sesame seed oil

1 cup chopped meat (you may use chicken, beef, or any meat of your choice)

Directions
In a large pot, combine the rice and water. Bring it to a boil on high heat, and then reduce the heat to a simmer. Cover and simmer for another 30 minutes.

Meanwhile in a large pan, heat the vegetable oil, then stir fry the bok choy. Transfer it to the pot with the rice. Add the other ingredients, and stir to combine.

Reduce the heat and cook for another 30 minutes. Let it cool, and serve.

Butternut Squash and Pomegranate Pie

Ingredients
1 cup butternut squash (cooked and pureed)

1 tablespoon orange juice

1 egg

½ cup pomegranate seeds

2 teaspoons arrowroot powder

1 tablespoon water

Directions
Preheat the oven to 300°F.

In a medium bowl, combine the squash, orange juice, egg, and pomegranate seeds. Mix well and set it aside.

In a saucepan on medium heat, combine the tablespoon of water and arrowroot powder, then whisk until it thickens. Add it to the squash mixture and combine it well.

Spread the mixture on a well-greased pie pan and bake for 30 to 40 minutes, or until it is separating from the pan. Allow it to cool, cut, then serve.

Puppy Moist Cake

Ingredients
1 egg

¼ cup vegetable oil

1 teaspoon vanilla extract

½ cup peanut butter

⅓ cup honey

1 cup carrots (shredded)

1 teaspoon baking soda

1 cup flour (you may use white or whole wheat)

Directions
Preheat the oven to 350°F and grease a small baking pan.

Using a medium-sized bowl, combine the egg, oil, vanilla, peanut butter, and honey. Mix well. Add the carrots and slowly add the baking soda and flour until it becomes thoroughly combined.

Transfer it to the baking pan, and bake for 30 to 40 minutes. Remove it from the oven and let it cool. Serve.

Puppy Meat Cake

Ingredients

3 cups water

1 ½ cups brown rice

2 large potatoes, grated

6 pounds ground beef

8 eggs

4 large carrots, grated

2 ribs celery, chopped

1 ½ cups rolled oats

Dash salt

¼ cup olive oil

Directions

Preheat the oven to 400°F, and grease 3 large muffin pans.

Mix the rice and water in a medium saucepan. Bring it to a boil on high heat, then reduce the heat and cook for another 20 to 30 minutes, covered. Remove it from the heat. Let it cool and fluff the rice using a fork.

Meanwhile, combine the potatoes, beef, eggs, carrots, and celery. Mix well, then add the oats, rice, salt, and olive oil. Combine thoroughly.

Scoop the mixture into the muffin pans. Make sure that it is firm. Bake for about 45 minutes. Remove the pans from the oven and let them cool. Turn the pan down to remove the cakes. Cut to serving pieces. You can freeze or refrigerate the leftovers.

Very Vegan Pup Food

Ingredients
1 large sweet potato

⅔ cups quinoa (uncooked)

1 ⅓ cups of water

1 banana, sliced

1 cup peas (frozen; cook as per package instructions)

Directions
Using a fork, pierce the sweet potato and cook it in the microwave until it is tender, about 15 minutes.

Meanwhile, bring the quinoa and water to a boil. Lower the heat, cover the pot, and continue simmering for around 15 minutes.

Chop the sweet potatoes to smaller pieces, then combine it with the cooked quinoa, banana, and peas. Serve.

Cranberry and Turkey Pupcakes

Ingredients

For the pupcakes

⅓ cup frozen and dried cranberries

½ cup hot water

1 egg

¼ cup pumpkin puree

1 pound lean ground turkey

For the frosting

3 tablespoons pumpkin puree

1 cup heavy whip cream

Cinnamon (just a dash)

Directions
Preheat the oven to 375°F, and grease a muffin pan.

Meanwhile, rehydrate the cranberries in the hot water for about 15 minutes.

Using a large mixing bowl, combine the egg, pumpkin puree, ground turkey, and cranberries. Mix until thoroughly combined.

Scoop the batter into the muffin cups. Bake for 25 to 30 minutes. Remove from the pan and let them cool.

To make the frosting, whip the cream with an electric mixer. Once you see that soft peaks are forming, add the puree and the cinnamon. Mix well. Frost the pupcakes, and serve.

Puppy Salad

Ingredients
⅓ cup brown rice (cooked)

1 cup carrots, grated

½ cup plain yogurt

¼ cup vegetable oil

Directions
Combine the rice and carrots in a medium-sized bowl, then set aside. In another bowl, combine the yogurt and vegetable oil. Mix all of the ingredients and toss. Serve about ¼ cup to your pup.

Store any leftovers in covered containers in the refrigerator. This can last for about 3 days.

Puppy Fruits and Veggie Mix

Ingredients
1 cup green peas

1 cup carrots

1 banana

Directions
Steam the peas and carrots until they are tender. Add the banana.

Place the mixture in a blender and puree for around 30 seconds. Serve.

You may also use other combinations:

2 bananas; 1 cup pumpkin puree, and 2 peaches

1 large pear; ½ cup grated carrots; 1 cup fresh spinach

1 apple; 1 cup green beans; 1 cup fresh lettuce

Recipes for Full Grown Dogs

Adult dogs have different needs from puppies, so they need a different amount of food. Here are nutritious recipes fit for your grown, active dogs!

Veggie and Turkey Casserole

Ingredients
1 ½ cups brown rice

1 tablespoon olive oil

3 pounds ground turkey

2 carrots (shredded)

½ cup peas (frozen or canned)

1 zucchini (shredded)

3 cups baby spinach (chopped)

Directions
In a large saucepan, boil 3 cups of water and cook the rice. Once it is cooked, set the rice aside.

Heat the olive oil on medium heat in a large stock pot. Cook the ground turkey until it becomes brown, about 3 to 5 minutes. Make sure that you crumble the turkey well.

Add the carrots and peas and cook for 5 minutes.

Add the cooked brown rice, zucchini, and spinach, and cook until the spinach becomes wilted, 3 to 5 minutes. Remove from heat and let it cool.

Veggie and Duck Raw Food

Ingredients
4 pounds duck wings

1 pound duck hearts (you can also use turkey hearts)

6 pounds of duck gizzards (you can also use venison)

1 ½ pounds of offal-organ blend (GreenTripe brand is a good choice)

1 pounds mixed frozen vegetables

Directions
Grind all the meat and place it in large steel bowls. Mix it all well together and then transfer it to plastic containers. Place them inside the refrigerator or freeze.

Once you are ready to feed your dogs with this meal, thaw the veggie mix and add it to the meat mixture. This food will last for about a week in the fridge, or longer in the freezer.

Slow-cooked Double Meat Surprise

Ingredients
1 ½ pounds boneless skinless chicken breast

1 ¼ pounds ground turkey

1 pound frozen peas

1 pound carrots, chopped

1 cup brown rice

2 apples (cored)

Directions

Place all the ingredients in a slow cooker, and add enough water to cover.

Cook for about 9 hours on low. Once it is done, stir the food.

Scoop out the veggies and mash them, and stir them back in with the meat mixture.

Divide the food into separate containers, and freeze or refrigerate.

Veggie and Beef Quinoa Balls

Ingredients
1 cup dry milk powder

1 cup cooked quinoa

2 (6 ounce) jars veggie and beef baby food (use organic as much as possible)

1 cup water

Directions
Preheat the oven to 350°F.

Combine all the ingredients in a large mixing bowl.

Scoop out some of the mixture, about the size of a large spoon, roll it onto a ball, and place it on a baking tray. Continue until all the mixture is used.

Bake for 12 to 15 minutes. Take them out of the oven and allow them to cool. Store the left-over balls in a container in the refrigerator. This will last for about 5 days.

Chicken Casserole

Ingredients

4 chicken breasts

½ cup chopped green beans

½ cup chopped broccoli

½ cup chopped carrots

½ cup rolled oats

4 cups low sodium chicken broth

Directions

Remove any extra fat from the breasts, and cut them into small chunks. Using a non-stick pan, cook the chicken on medium heat until it is not pink anymore. You can add a bit of olive oil in frying your chicken if it is sticking on the pan.

Combine the chicken, veggies, rolled oats, and broth in a large pot. Cook on medium heat for around 15 minutes, or until the carrots are tender.

Store the leftovers in a container in the refrigerator. This will last for about 5 days.

Chili Dog for Your Doggie

Ingredients

4 chicken breasts

1 cup kidney beans (drained)

1 cup black beans (drained)

1 cup diced carrots

½ cup tomato paste

4 cups chicken broth

2 teaspoons fish oil

Directions

Remove any extra fat from the breasts and cut them into small chunks. In a non-stick pan, cook the chicken on medium heat until it is not pink anymore.

Combine the chicken, beans, carrots, tomato paste, and broth in a pot on medium heat for around 10 minutes, until the veggies are tender. Last, stir in the fish oil.

Once cooked, remove the pot from the heat and allow it to cool before giving it to your dog.

Store the leftover chili in your refrigerator. This will last for about 5 days.

Doggie-friendly Beef Stew

Ingredients
1 small sweet potato

2-4 tablespoons olive oil

1 pound stew beef

½ cup flour

½ cup water

½ cup green beans, chopped

½ cup carrots, diced

Directions
Pierce the sweet potato with a fork and cook it in the microwave for around 5-8 minutes until it becomes firm but tender. Set it aside.

Meanwhile, cut the beef into smaller cubes and brown it in the olive oil over medium heat.

Remove the beef from the pan and reserve the drippings.

Meanwhile, dice the sweet potatoes.

Heat the meat drippings on medium heat and the add flour slowly, together with the water. Whisk until it creates a thick consistency and becomes gravy. (You can also choose to buy ready-made gravy instead, if it is free of additives.)

Add the meat, green beans, carrots, and sweet potato to the gravy mixture, and make sure that it is coated fully. Cook for around 10 minutes or until the carrots are tender. Cool first, then serve.

You can store the leftovers in a container in the refrigerator. This will last for about 5 days.

Doggie Chicken Dinner

Ingredients

5 pounds chicken (you can use the whole chicken including heart, liver and neck meat)

4 cups chicken broth

2 apples (peeled and cored)

2 cups red cabbage

2 cups spinach

2 tablespoons olive oil

5 eggs (cooked or raw)

Directions

Chop the chicken and cook it with the chicken broth in a large pot until fully cooked. Reduce the heat and simmer.

Add the apples, cabbage, and spinach. Simmer more until the apples and veggies are fully cooked. Remove the pot from the heat and let it cool.

Add the olive oil and eggs then stir. Serve to your dog.

You can store the leftovers in a container in the refrigerator. This will last for about 5 days.

Fish Dinner

Ingredients

3 cups diced veggies

2 cups water

1-2 cans salmon

2 pounds fish fillets (fresh or frozen)

3 eggs (cooked or raw)

1 cup cooked rice (brown or white)

Directions

Combine the vegetables with the water in a medium saucepan. When they have softened, add the fish and cook over medium-low heat until the fish is cooked. Break it up well with a wooden spoon.

Remove the pot from the heat and stir in the eggs and rice. Let it cool. You can keep the leftovers in the refrigerator for about 3 days.

Rice, Broccoli, and Chicken Doggie Dinner

Ingredients

5 pounds chicken (diced)

2 cups water

5 cups rice (cooked; brown or white)

3 tablespoons olive oil

5 eggs (cooked or raw)

3 cups broccoli, chopped

Directions

Simmer the chicken in the water until it is cooked. Add the rice.

Stir in the broccoli, and leave it on the heat until the broccoli is cooked.

Once cooked, let it cool then add the eggs with the oil.

Leftovers can be kept in the fridge for about 5 days.

Doggie Beef Dinner

Ingredients

10 pounds ground beef (you may also use ground turkey)

2 tablespoons olive oil

5 cups rice (cooked; brown or white)

10 eggs (cooked or raw)

3 cups mixed veggies

Directions

This recipe can be prepared in 2 ways:
First: heat the olive oil and brown the meat. Add the rice, eggs, and veggies and cook until they are soft, then let it cool and serve.

Second: combine all the ingredients except the meat. Cook with a bit of water until soft, then add the raw meat. Mix well. Form the mixture into meatballs and cook them in the oven at 400°F for 45 minutes, or until it is cooked.

Slow Cooker Chicken and Brown Rice

Ingredients

2 cups water

1 cup brown rice

3 medium carrots

1 medium-sized sweet potato

2 pieces of chicken (boneless)

Directions

Place all of the ingredients in your slow cooker. Cook for about 4 to 5 hours on the high heat setting.

Once the chicken is cooked, cut or shred it into small pieces.

Refrigerate any leftovers in an airtight container. This can last for about 3 to 4 days.

Surprise Turkey Rice

Ingredients

1 pound ground turkey

2 cups brown rice

6 cups water

1 teaspoon dried rosemary

½ cup carrots

½ cup broccoli

½ cup cauliflower

Directions

Put the turkey, rice, water, and rosemary in a large pot. Stir well until the turkey separates.

Bring it to a boil, then reduce the heat. Simmer for about 20 minutes, then add the veggies and cook for another 5 minutes. Let it cool then serve.

Hearty and Healthy Meatballs

Ingredients

1 tablespoon parsley flakes

2 tablespoons Omega oil (3 and 6)

¼ cup honey

½ pound ground beef

½ cup apples (grated)

Olive oil, for frying

Directions

Combine all the ingredients and shape them to balls.

Bake or fry them using olive oil. Let them cool, then serve.

Doggie Fishy Dinner

Ingredients

1 can salmon

1 egg

3 tablespoons flour

1 tablespoon olive oil

1 medium potato

1 medium carrot

1 piece of celery

Directions

Drain the liquid from the salmon and make sure it is dry. Mix in the egg and flour, and form small patties.

Fry the patties and remove them from the oil.

Chop all the veggies into small pieces.

Add the veggies and cook them in the oil for 5 to 8 minutes, then serve.

Healthy Quinoa and Chicken Salad for Dogs

Ingredients

1 cup quinoa

2 cups water

½ pound chicken (boneless)

3 cups kale (chopped)

2 zucchinis

3 handfuls of green beans

Directions
Cook the quinoa in the water as per package instructions.

Meanwhile, slice the chicken into serving strips. Cook it in the olive oil until it is browned, and then add veggies and cook.

Stir in the quinoa until thoroughly mixed, then serve.

Doggie Lamb Stew

Ingredients
½ cup carrots, grated

2 cups ground lamb

2 ½ cups water

1 cup brown rice (cooked)

½ cup yogurt (fat-free)

Directions
Place the carrots, lamb, and water in a medium-sized pot. Cover and cook on low heat until the lamb is cooked. Break the pieces up with a wooden spoon.

Let the mixture cool down, and add the brown rice and yogurt. Serve.

Doggie Liver Loaf

Ingredients

2 large eggs

1 pound chicken liver

1 tablespoon brown sugar

1 ½ cups cornmeal

Directions

Preheat the oven to 400°F.

Puree the eggs, liver, and brown sugar using a food processor. Make sure that it is blended well.

Mix in the cornmeal.

Pour the mixture in a greased baking pan (9x9 inches). Bake until cooked, 25 to 30 minutes. If a knife inserted in the center comes out clean, it is cooked through.

Cut into serving pieces.

Best Doggie Burger

Ingredients

½ pound ground beef or turkey

1 or 2 medium potatoes

½ a bag of baby carrots (you may also use ½ cup of grated carrots)

Directions

Shape the ground meat into patties, and grill it until it is cooked well.

Meanwhile, cook the potatoes until they are soft, then mash them. Shape them like a patty as well, then prepare them like a burger sandwich.

Add carrots on the side, then serve.

Delish Turkey Scramble

Ingredients

1 egg

1-2 tablespoons mashed potato

½ cup turkey meat (cooked and diced)

½ cup veggies

Directions

Mix the eggs and mashed potatoes together.

Heat the oil in a medium skillet. Add the mixture, along with the turkey and veggies.

Cook and stir until the egg is cooked. Serve.

Awesome Lamb Lunch

Ingredients
2 eggs (beaten)

1 ½ cups lamb meat (chopped to small pieces and already cooked)

3 cups rice (cooked; you may use brown or white)

¼ cup plain yogurt

Directions
Mix all the ingredients together except the yogurt. Cook in the microwave for 2 to 3 minutes until the eggs are cooked.

Stir well, then add the yogurt. Serve.

Quick Raw Dog Chow

Ingredients
2 cup meats of your choice

½ cup cottage cheese

Directions
Mix all of the ingredients well then serve.

Mexican Chicken Stew

Ingredients

4 pieces boneless skinless chicken breasts or 8-10 chicken thighs (you may also use 4 turkey thighs)

1 tablespoon olive oil

2 cups chicken or beef broth

1 small cabbage

3 large carrots

1 red bell pepper

1 medium sweet potato

3 small potatoes

2 small rutabagas

Sprigs of cilantro

Cumin to taste

Directions

In a large heavy pot, sauté the chicken in the olive oil, and sprinkle in a bit of cumin. Remove it from the heat, and set it aside.

Using the same pot, mix together all the other ingredients. Simmer for 15 to 20 minutes, and add cooked the chicken. Cover and continue simmering.

Once all the veggies are cooked, remove the pot from the heat. Let cool, then serve.

Stew Raw Mix

Ingredients

2 cups veggies of your choice (pureed)

2 to 4 ounces of organ meat of your choice (raw)

1 pound of ground meat of your choice (raw)

½ cup apple cider vinegar

½ cup of yogurt (plain)

Handful of parsley

1 tablespoon kelp (ground)

3 eggs

Directions
Combine all the ingredients and mix well. Form the mixture into balls or patties depending on your preference.

Store in the freezer or refrigerator until ready to serve.

Buffalo Loaf

Ingredients

2 eggs

3 cups ground lean buffalo meat

¾ cups veggies of your choice (chopped)

1 ½ cup rolled oats

½ cup cottage cheese

Directions

Preheat the oven to 350°F.

Meanwhile, mix all the ingredients and put them in a well-greased baking pan. Bake the mixture for 40 minutes, and check if the middle is cooked.

Let it cool, then serve.

Recipes for Lactating Dogs

Lactating dogs need more nutrition since they are producing milk and taking care of their young. Lactating or nursing dogs must have extra calories, and they require more protein, phosphorus, and calcium. Here are some recipes which will help them heal faster from the birth, and at the same time provide the best nutrition for their young pups.

You can also feed your very active dog with these nutrient-rich recipes.

Rice with Fish and Beef

Ingredients

4 pounds ground beef

6 eggs

1 sweet potato

4 cups carrots and peas

1 can mackerel (drained)

1 tablespoon fresh rosemary (chopped finely)

1 tablespoon ginger (chopped finely)

1 ⅓ cup white rice (cooked)

Directions

Sauté the ground beef until it is cooked. Drain any extra grease. Beat the eggs lightly and add them to the beef. Stir until cooked through.

Pierce the sweet potato and microwave it for around 10 minutes, or until it becomes soft. Mash it and add it to the skillet with the beef.

Steam the veggies, then mash them lightly. Add the rosemary, ginger and the drained mackerel. Stir them into the beef mixture.

Add the rice and heat together. Serve.

Fishy Fry

Ingredients

2 pounds white fish (such as cod)

1 tablespoon olive oil

½ cup peas

½ cup green beans

1 cup zucchini

2 cans pink salmon

2 eggs

Directions

In a medium skillet, cook the fish in the olive oil. Add the veggies, and sauté until the vegetables become soft.

Add the salmon and eggs, and mix them together with the white fish and veggies. Serve.

Sweet Potato with Chicken and Sage

Ingredients

2 pounds lean chicken

2 sweet potatoes

½ pound spinach

15 sage leaves (or half a package)

4 tablespoons olive oil

Directions

Boil the chicken until it is cooked through, and shred it with two forks.

Meanwhile, pierce the sweet potato and microwave it for about 10 minutes.

Over low to medium heat, heat the oil in a frying pan and add the sage leaves. Cook for around 2 minutes, and add the spinach and cook until it becomes wilted. Once done, the rest of the ingredients including the chicken, and cook for 2 more minutes. Remove it from the heat, and let it cool. Serve.

Beef and Eggs

Ingredients

2 pounds ground beef

¼ cup powdered kelp

Bunch of kale

1 cup chicken or beef broth

5 eggs, lightly beaten

Directions
Cook the beef completely and drain any excess grease. Add the kelp and kale with the broth. Simmer for around 5 minutes.

Pour in the eggs and cook until they are set. Let it cool. Serve.

Baked Chili and Cheese

Ingredients
2 tablespoons butter

1 pound ground beef

1 small can corn

1 small can tomato paste

4 carrots

2 pounds dry macaroni (cooked as per package directions)

1 cup mozzarella cheese

8 ounces cream cheese

More cheese of your choice, shredded

Directions
Melt the butter and cook the beef, corn, tomato paste, and carrots for around 5 minutes. Remove it from the heat.

Preheat the oven to 350°F. Pour the cooked macaroni in a 9x13 baking pan. To the skillet, add the mozzarella cheese and cream cheese. Mix well

Pour the mixture over the macaroni, then add the broth and sprinkle more cheese on top. Bake for 30 minutes.

Let it cool, and serve.

Chicken with oats

Ingredients
1 cup rice

2 ½ cups water

2 pounds boneless chicken breast (chopped)

½ cup carrots, diced

2 cups of spinach

½ cup plain yogurt

½ cup parsley (chopped)

2 tablespoons olive oil

⅔ cups quick oats

Directions
In a medium saucepan, boil the water and cook the rice, chicken, and carrots until they are done.

Remove the chicken to a cutting board, and shred it with two forks.

Stir the spinach into the hot rice mixture, and let it sit until it is wilted.

Mix in the yogurt, parsley, olive oil, and oats.

Form the mixture into balls or patties. Place them in the refrigerator until they have cooled. Serve.

Salmon Medley

Ingredients

2 pounds salmon (you can either use fresh or canned)

2 cups rice, cooked

½ cup cauliflower

1 cup peas

Directions

Bake the salmon (if using fresh) for 5 to 10 minutes at 350°F. Once cooked, set it aside to cool.

Shred the fish and place it in a mixing bowl.

Steam the cauliflower and peas.

Combine all the ingredients well, then serve.

Tuna Balls

Ingredients

1 cup rice

2 cups water

4 eggs

½ pound spinach

2 pounds canned tuna

2-3 tablespoons bread crumbs

Coconut oil

Directions
Boil the water and cook the rice until firm. Add the spinach and eggs, and heat through until the eggs are completely cooked and the spinach is wilted. Add all the other ingredients.

Form the mixture into balls. Place them in the refrigerator until they are set. Serve.

Triple Treat

Ingredients
1 pound ground beef

1 pound ground or chopped chicken

½ pound carrots

1 cup peas

2 cups broccoli

1 pound salmon (canned)

Directions
Sauté the beef and chicken until they are completely done.

Meanwhile, steam the carrots, peas, and broccoli.

Combine all the ingredients, then serve.

Yogurty Chicken

Ingredients

1 pound chicken

½ cup spinach

1 cup plain yogurt

½ can pumpkin puree

Directions

Boil the chicken until it is completely cooked. Remove it to a cutting board and shred it with two forks.

Chop the spinach, and mix it with the hot chicken until it wilts.

Mix in the other ingredients, then serve.

Mix It All Up Doggie Food

Ingredients

2 pounds ground pork

2 pounds ground beef

1 ½ cups water

1 cup rice

½ cup blueberries

1 large apple, cored

1 large sweet potato

2 carrots

1 cup kale

Directions

Place the beef and pork in a slow cooker. Stir in the water, rice, and blueberries.

Chop the apple, sweet potato, and carrots into 1-inch cubes, and chop the kale. Add them all to the slow cooker, and cook on high for 3 to 5 hours, or on low for 5 to 7 hours, until the meat is cooked through.

Bone Broth Doggie Treat

Ingredients

1 sweet potato

2 apples (seeds removed and cored)

1 cup bone broth

6 chicken livers

¾ cup ground flaxseed (you may also use hemp meal or pumpkin seed)

Vitamin A supplement (optional)

Directions

Combine the ingredients in a slow cooker and cook until all are soft, 4-5 hours on low, or 6 hours on high. Allow the mixture to cool.

Once it has cooled, purée until smooth. Spoon it into molds, then freeze.

Doggie Risotto

Ingredients

1 potato, diced

1 tablespoon olive oil

½ cup rice (whole grain, cooked)

3 ounces chicken, cooked and diced

½ cup sweet corn

Kale, chopped

2 tablespoons plain yogurt

1 teaspoon sesame oil

Directions

Heat the olive oil, and cook the potatoes until they are translucent.

Add the rice, chicken, corn, and kale, and stir.

Reduce the heat, and mix in the yogurt. Cook for another 5 minutes, while continuously stirring.

Allow the mixture to cool, and add a few drops of sesame oil before serving.

Double Meaty Slow Cooker Meal

Ingredients

1 ½ pounds chicken breast

2 apples, seeded and cored

1 pound frozen peas

1 pound carrots

1 pound ground turkey

1 cup brown rice

Directions

Place all the ingredients in the slow cooker. Add water to completely cover everything.

Cook for around 9 hours on low. Check, and stir together. Serve.

Turkey with Rosemary Stew

Ingredients
6 cups water

2 cups brown rice

1 tablespoon olive oil

1 pound ground turkey

1 teaspoon dried rosemary

2 cups mixed vegetables (such as cauliflower, carrots, and broccoli)

Directions

In a medium saucepan, bring the water to a boil, and cook the rice until it is tender. Drain any excess water and set aside.

In a medium skillet, heat the olive oil and cook the turkey until it is browned. Mix in the rosemary and the veggies.

Stir in the rice, and serve.

Ingredients

1 ½ pounds potatoes, peeled and shredded

3 tablespoons butter

¾ pound corned beef, chopped

½ cup carrots, shredded

Black pepper

½ cup cream

4 eggs (cooked according to your preference)

4 slices toast (lightly buttered)

Directions

Place the potatoes in a colander and salt them lightly. Drain for a few minutes.

In a large, nonstick pan, melt the butter. Add the potatoes, corned beef, and carrots. Cook on medium-high heat, and place a plate on top to weigh it down and allow a crust to form.

Cook for around 15 minutes, or until the potatoes are tender. Season with pepper and add the cream.

Place a cooked egg on top of the hash, and serve with toast.

Meatballs and Pasta

Ingredients

6 cups chicken broth

¾ pound ground pork, veal or beef (or a combination)

⅓ cup carrots, shredded

2 large eggs

⅓ cup Parmesan cheese, plus more for garnish

¼ cup parsley, finely chopped finely

⅓ cup bread crumbs

Black pepper

½ pound ditalini pasta

Directions

In a deep saucepan, bring the broth to a simmer.

In a medium-sized bowl, combine the meat, carrots, eggs, Parmesan, parsley, bread crumbs, and pepper. Mix well, and then form the paste into 1-inch balls (smaller for small dogs).

Carefully lower the meatballs into the simmering broth, and cook for around 5 minutes. Add the pasta and let it cook until it becomes al dente, around 7 minutes.

Let it cool, and sprinkle some more Parmesan cheese on top before serving.

Awesome Salmon Cakes

Ingredients

½ cup breadcrumbs (you may also use cracker meal)

1 (6 ounce) can of salmon, drained

1 large egg, beaten

1 tablespoon fresh dill, chopped

¼ red bell pepper, finely chopped

1 tablespoon olive oil

Directions

In a medium-sized bowl, mix the breadcrumbs or cracker meal with the salmon. Add the egg, dill, and bell pepper. If the mixture is too wet, add more breadcrumbs or cracker meal. Form the mixture into patties.

Heat the oil in a medium-sized pan. Add the salmon patties and cook them for 3 minutes on each side, or until they are nicely browned.

Let them cool, and serve.

Breakfast Pancakes

Ingredients

1 cup milk

1 tablespoon honey

1 ½ tablespoons butter, melted

2 eggs

½ cup all-purpose flour

1 cup whole wheat flour

½ teaspoon ground cinnamon

1 teaspoon baking powder

2 cups sliced or small fruits (berries, banana, and mango)

Cooking spray

½ cup plain yogurt

Directions

In a medium-sized bowl, combine the milk, honey, butter, honey, and eggs. In increments, add both flours, cinnamon, and baking powder.

Spray some cooking oil on your griddle. Pour 2 tablespoons of the batter and cook until you see bubbles beginning to show on top. Add some of the fruit on top, and then flip. Cook for around 2 minutes, and then transfer the cooked pancakes to a plate. Drizzle with yogurt, then add the remaining fruit.

Baked Hashed Sweet Potatoes and Eggs

Ingredients

1 medium sweet potato

1 tablespoon olive oil

2 medium beets, boiled

4 eggs

Directions
Preheat the oven to 350°F.

Grate the sweet potatoes, and press out as much of the moisture as you can into a clean kitchen towel.

In a large skillet, heat the olive oil on medium-high heat. Add the sweet potatoes. Mix well and cook until they become soft and brown.

Grease a 9x9 baking pan. Slice the beets and arrange them in the pan to create the crust. Spoon the sweet potato hash on top. Create holes to provide space for your eggs.

Crack the eggs on the hash and bake for 15 to 20 minutes.

Chicken, Mushroom & Bacon Quiche

Ingredients
2 ounces dried mushrooms

1 teaspoon coconut oil

6 strips bacon, chopped

1 ½ cups chicken, cooked (leftovers are great)

2 teaspoons dried sage

6 eggs

1 cup full fat coconut milk

Directions

Place the dried mushrooms in a bowl and cover them with hot water. Let them sit for around 30 minutes. Once they are softened, drain them well.

Preheat the oven to 375°F, and grease a 9x13 glass baking dish with the coconut oil.

In a large pan, brown the bacon and drain the fat. Add the leftover chicken, sage, and mushrooms, and cook for a few minutes, until the liquid evaporates. Place the mixture in the baking dish.

Crack the eggs into a medium-sized bowl, and add the coconut milk. Whisk to combine completely, then pour it over the mushroom mixture in the baking pan.

Bake for around 30 minutes, or until you will see that the center is completely set. Take out of the oven, and serve.

Pumpkin & Beef Stew

Ingredients
1 tablespoon coconut oil, divided

1 pound ground beef

3 zucchini, diced

4 cups beef stock (choose the variety with low sodium)

3 cups tomato sauce

2 cups pumpkin puree

2 teaspoons oregano

Directions

In a large Dutch oven or heavy-bottomed pan, melt half the coconut oil over medium heat. Brown the ground beef for 3 to 5 minutes. Once the beef is completely browned, remove it from the pan and set it aside.

Melt the remaining coconut oil. Sauté the zucchini about 5 minutes, or until it is slightly soft.

Add a few splashes of stock and scrape the bottom of the pan for the drippings. Add the beef back to the pan, together with the tomato sauce and pumpkin puree. Stir to combine completely. Add the remaining stock and oregano.

Reduce the heat and simmer for about 15-20 minutes to thicken.

Allow the mixture to cool a little before serving.

Minestrone and Macaroni Soup

Ingredients

2 tablespoons olive oil

1 red bell pepper, diced

1 green bell pepper, diced

1 zucchini, diced

½ cup mushrooms, sliced

4 cups beef stock

1 cup uncooked macaroni

1 can white beans, drained

1 pack frozen mixed vegetables (small size)

Fresh basil for garnish (chopped)

Directions

Heat the oil in a pot, and add the red and green bell peppers, zucchini, and mushrooms. Add the beef stock and bring it to a boil. Reduce the heat.

Add the macaroni pasta and cook until it is done.

Add the beans and the frozen vegetables, and simmer for a few more minutes.

Serve warm with chopped fresh basil on top.

Herbed Beef Roast

Ingredients

1 pound beef precooked roast au jus

1 pound small red potatoes, quartered

3 carrots, peeled and sliced diagonally

1 tablespoon cooking oil

Black pepper to taste

3 tablespoons fresh flatleaf parsley, chopped

1 tablespoon lemon peel, finely shredded

Directions

Cook the beef roast, covered, in a large skillet over medium-high heat for about 10 minutes. Once done, simmer for another 5 minutes until its juices are reduced slightly.

Place the quartered potatoes and sliced carrots in a microwave-safe dish. Drizzle the vegetables with oil and season with pepper. Toss slightly to even out the flavor and oil. Cover, and cook in the microwave oven on high for about 10 minutes, until tender.

In a small bowl, combine the parsley and lemon peel, and set aside.

Stir the vegetables into the skillet with the beef roast. Add the herb mixture. Serve.

Brown Rice and Beef Soup

Ingredients

1 tablespoon canola oil

2 pounds stew beef

½ cup carrots, chopped

½ cup celery, chopped

12 cups water

1 cup dry brown rice

Directions

Heat the oil in a very large, thick-bottomed pot until hot. Working in batches, sear the beef and set it aside on a plate.

Using the same pot, sauté the carrots and celery. Add the beef back into the pot and pour in the water. Simmer until the meat becomes soft and tender.

Skim any excess fat on top of the pot.

Add the brown rice. Simmer for 30 minutes, or until the rice is thoroughly cooked.

Vegetarian Dog Food Recipes

Just like us human beings, dogs also need vegetables in their daily meals. However, this should not surpass 10% of their total food requirement, in order to maintain a balanced diet.

Vegetable Stew

Ingredients
3 tablespoons olive oil

1 potato, peeled and cubed

1 medium zucchini, sliced

1 medium yellow squash, peeled and sliced

1 medium eggplant

2 cups water

1 tablespoon oregano or basil

Salt and pepper for seasoning

Directions
Heat the oil in a large Dutch oven. Add the potato, and fry it for about 2 minutes. Add the zucchini, squash, and eggplant, and cook for 2 more minutes, or until all the vegetables begin to soften.

Pour in the water, and bring the mixture to a boil. Reduce the heat and let it simmer for about 30 minutes, or until all vegetables are well cooked. Add the oregano or basil, salt and pepper. Pour the stew into a bowl and let it cool down before serving.

Dog Bulgur Biscuits

Ingredients

3 cups whole wheat flour

3 cups all-purpose flour

2 cups bulgur wheat

1 cup cornmeal

3 cups chicken broth

Directions

Preheat the oven to 300°F.

In a large bowl, mix the flours, wheat, and cornmeal.

Pour the chicken broth into the mixture, and combine until a firm dough is formed.

Lightly flour the working surface and a rolling pin. Roll the dough to at least ¼ inch thick, and cut it into the desired shapes.

Arranged the pieces one inch apart on an ungreased baking tray, and bake for 40-45 minutes. Allow them to cool completely before storing them in an airtight container.

Veggie Vittles

Ingredients

1 tablespoon brewer's yeast

1 cup cooked rice

1 cup vegetables, may be cooked, cubed, or mashed

⅓ cup applesauce

1 egg, beaten

Directions

Preheat the oven to 350°F.

Combine all the ingredients in a medium-sized bowl and mix well.

Scoop out a heaping teaspoon of the dough, and shape it into a biscuit. Repeat until all the dough is used.

Arrange the treats on a greased baking pan, and bake for 12 minutes, or until golden brown.

Once cooled, transfer the treats to an airtight container and refrigerate overnight.

Dog Treat Recipes

We love to give our dogs delicious treats every now and then. Whenever we train them, take them for a walk, when traveling, and especially if they behave, we make sure that they are awarded with their favorite dog biscuits. These delicious biscuits would definitely make your dog enjoy your bonding and all the more, and you'll know they're good for your pet because they were made with love by you. Here are some easy to make dog biscuit recipes you and your dog will surely like.

Beef Biscuits

Ingredients
2 cups whole wheat or all-purpose flour

1 large egg, beaten

1 cup corn meal

¼ cup wheat germ

1 tablespoon cooking oil

2 teaspoons beef bouillon powder

1 cup hot water

Directions
Preheat the oven to 285°F.

In a medium-sized bowl, mix all the ingredients and mix them together until they are well blended. Make sure any lumps of wheat are properly mixed.

Scoop out spoonfuls of dough and shape round biscuit discs. Arrange them on an ungreased baking pan.

Bake for 2 hours, or until the biscuits are golden brown. Let them cool completely, and store them in an airtight container.

Rufus's Favorite Biscuits

Ingredients
Bouillon cubes (chicken or beef)

½ cup hot water

½ cup meat drippings

2 cups rolled oats

3 ½ cups whole wheat flour

Directions:
Preheat the oven to 300°F.

In a small bowl, dissolve the bouillon cubes in the hot water. Add the meat drippings and set the mixture aside.

In another medium-sized bowl, combine the oatmeal and flour, and mix well.

Combine the wet and dry ingredients and mix until it is smooth and thick.

Roll out the dough and cut it into the desired shapes. Arrange them on the baking pan.

Bake for an hour, or until the biscuits are golden brown. Turn off the oven, and let the biscuits harden inside the oven. Store them in an airtight container when they are cool.

Liver Biscuits

Ingredients
1 pound beef liver

½ teaspoon lemon juice

1 cup cornmeal

1 ½ cups whole wheat flour

Directions
Preheat the oven to 350°F. Prepare a baking pan with oil or cooking spray.

Puree the beef liver in a food processor and pour it in a large bowl.

Stir in the lemon juice to reduce the strong smell, and then add the cornmeal. Stir in the wheat flour little by little, and mix well.

Spread the mixture evenly in the greased baking pan. Bake the biscuits for 20 minutes. Let the mixture cool down for an hour or two, and then cut it into cubes and refrigerate afterwards.

Quick and Easy Dog Treat Recipes

No matter how much we try to plan our daily activities, such as walking our dog early in the morning, leaving for work, spending time with our dog when we come back, and then walking with him in the evening, there are just things that you cannot control. Traffic, deadlines, and unexpected happenings. In these hectic moments there might be times when we don't have an hour to spare to prepare our dogs their meal for tomorrow, so we might simply rely on the commercial dog food at the market. But that's not your only option! Here are some easy dog food recipes for on-the-go persons like you.

Cinnamon Chicken Treats

Ingredients
1 cup chicken broth

¼ cup cornstarch

1 cup flour

¾ cup rolled oats

1 tablespoon baking powder

¼ cup vegetable oil

2 tablespoons cinnamon

Directions
Preheat the oven to 350°F. Prepare a baking sheet with cooking spray or oil.

In a large bowl, mix all the ingredients together until a smooth dough is formed. Spread the mixture on the prepared sheet and bake it for 15-20 minutes, or until the dough is golden brown.

Let it cool down, and cut it into squares. Refrigerate afterwards.

Prince's Liver Treat

Ingredients

2 cups cornmeal

1 pound beef liver, puréed

1 cup all-purpose flour

A dash of salt

Directions

Preheat the oven to 350°F. Prepare a cookie sheet with cooking spray or oil.

Mix all the ingredients together in a medium-sized bowl to make a dough. Make sure there are no lumps.

Spread the mixture on the prepared cookie sheet in a thin, even layer.

Bake for 15-20 minutes. Let it cool down and then cut it into cubes, or any shapes you desire.

Cold Yogurt with Peanut Butter Treats

Ingredients

1 cup peanut butter

4 cups plain yogurt

Directions

Place the peanut butter in a microwaveable dish and heat it until the peanut butter melts.

Pour the melted peanut butter into a bowl, and mix it with the yogurt.

Pour the mixture into cupcake papers, and refrigerate afterwards.

15 Minute Liver Treats

Ingredients

1 pound chicken livers

2 cups chicken broth

1 egg, beaten

1 cup cornmeal

1 cup all-purpose or whole wheat flour

Salt and pepper

Directions

Preheat the oven to 400°F, and prepare a baking sheet with cooking spray.

In a blender, process the chicken livers with the chicken broth and blend until it liquefies.

Add the beaten egg to the blender and let it blend for a minute. Pour the mixture into a medium-sized bowl.

Add the cornmeal and then, slowly, the flour. Lastly, add a pinch of salt and pepper.

Mix well until no lumps of flour are seen in the dough.

Pour the mixture onto the prepared baking pan, and bake it for 15 minutes. While it is still warm, cut the baked treats into the desired shape. Refrigerate afterwards.

Milky Bone Dog Biscuits

Ingredients
2 tablespoons powdered milk

¾ cup hot water

1 teaspoon salt

1 egg, beaten

3 cups whole wheat flour

Directions
Preheat the oven to 325°F.

In a medium-sized bowl, pour the powdered milk and dilute it with hot water. Stir in the salt and the egg.

Slowly add the flour into the solution, and knead for 2 or 3 minutes, until a smooth dough is formed.

Roll out the dough and cut bone-shaped treats. Bake for 40 to 50 minutes, or until the dough is firm and golden brown.

Cool the treats completely. Store them in an airtight container in the fridge.

Happy Dog Bones

Ingredients
2 cups whole wheat flour

1 cup cornmeal

2 cups soy flour

1 cup yeast flakes

1 cup wheat germ

1 egg, beaten

½ cup cooking oil

1 ¾ cups broth (or water)

Directions
Preheat the oven to 325°F.

In a large bowl, combine all the dry ingredients and make sure they are well mixed.

In a separate bowl, combine the egg, cooking oil and broth or water.

Blend all the ingredients together until a smooth dough is formed. Then portion the dough into thirds, and roll it out on a floured surface to a ¼-inch thickness.

Cut the dough in bone shapes and bake for 30 minutes. When done, let it cool down then refrigerate afterwards.

Princess's Bone Biscuits

Ingredients

2 tablespoons wheat germ

2 tablespoons soy flour

2 cups whole wheat flour

½ teaspoon salt

2 eggs, beaten

4 tablespoons cold water

Directions

Preheat the oven to 325°F.

Mix all the dry ingredients together in a large bowl.

Add the beaten eggs and cold water and combine until a dough is formed. Knead the dough for 3 minutes, and make sure that no lumps of flour are left.

Roll out the dough and cut it into dog bone shapes. Arrange it on a greased cookie sheet, and bake for 25 minutes.

Let the biscuits cool down, then refrigerate.

Gourmet Dog Food Recipes

Who said only humans can enjoy gourmet dishes? Even our dogs can have a taste of gourmet food as well. And no, I'm not talking about your leftovers from your dinner in the fancy restaurant. What I'm meaning to say is a canine version of a gourmet dish. "Gourmet" dog food doesn't have to be extra expensive with a fancy presentation. Gourmet dog food is just a way for dog lovers like you to show how much you appreciate your dog. And not only that, these recipes would also be perfect for celebrating your dog's birthday, and other canine special occasions.

Divine Doggy Dinner

Ingredients

½ pound ground beef (you may also use chicken, lamb, or turkey)

¼ cup rice, cooked

1 small potato, peeled

½ carrot, chopped

¼ teaspoon salt

1 small banana, peeled and mashed

Directions

Preheat a medium skillet and sauté the meat until it is browned.

Drain all the fat in the pan and stir in the rice with it. Transfer the mixture to a medium-sized bowl and set it aside.

Place the vegetables it in a pot of boiling water, and let them simmer for 15 minutes, or until they are tender, and drain the water.

Add the vegetables to the bowl of meat and rice and add the salt. Allow the mixture to cool a bit, and then stir in the banana.

Chinese Dog Food Recipe

Ingredients
3 teaspoons soy sauce

6 eggs, beaten

1 cup chicken stock

3 teaspoons cornstarch

2 tablespoons vegetable oil

⅓ cup celery, chopped

⅓ cup baby cabbage, finely chopped

1 cup ground beef, pre-cooked (may use flaked fish instead)

Directions
In a small bowl, combine the soy sauce and beaten eggs, and mix well.

In a separate small bowl, mix the chicken stock with the cornstarch, little by little. When the mixture is sticky and no lumps of cornstarch can be seen, set it aside.

Preheat your frying pan over medium-low heat, and pour in the vegetable oil. Sauté the celery and baby cabbage until they are tender.

Add the pre-cooked meat or flaked fish to the pan, and stir-fry for another 3 minutes. Add more oil if necessary. When the meat or fish is well mixed with the vegetables, transfer the mixture to a bowl and set it aside.

In the same pan, scramble the egg mixture until it is cooked. Pour in the stock and add the cooked vegetables and meat. Mix well until blended.

When the eggs are fully cooked and the stock had been absorbed by the meat and vegetables, pour it into a separate bowl and let it cool down before serving.

Parting Words

Now that you know how to prepare healthy meals for your dog, I am quite sure he will never have looked as healthy and energetic as he is right now. But just because you have finished reading this book, doesn't mean that your whole adventure in the kitchen and the lovely meals your dog is having is over. You can still try many combinations of these meals for breakfast, lunch, dinner, and snacks for your dog to enjoy. And you do not have to worry that your dog will ever be bored with your creations, because you have such a variety of recipes to choose from.

You may also try varying the ingredients in these dog food recipes – as long as you avoid the foods listed in Chapter Two that are not good for your dog – to create a new version of the meals. Just think about all the possibilities! Your dog will be even more excited to eat up when you call his name for dinner, because he knows that his meal would not only be delicious, but it is also made with love by you.

Cooking your dog's food does not only allow you to make sure that he is getting the right combination of food to achieve a balanced diet, but you are also building an even stronger relationship with your dog. As they say, if getting to a man's heart is through his stomach, capturing your dog's loyalty is through his meals as well, because building a strong relationship with your dog does not only require having playtime with him every day, but also promoting his good health. For even if he wants to play with you for a long time, without enough energy from the food he eats, he cannot do so. Thus, serving him meals made by you is another activity that you and especially your dog may enjoy.

Just keep in mind not to overcook the food. As you know, the more you cook food, the less nutritious it becomes, and you wouldn't want to deprive your dog of the nutrition he needs from his meals. You should still be attentive to the needs of your dog; just because you are serving him nutritious and delicious food, that doesn't mean that he can't get sick. He still needs to have his regular visit with his vet, and never forget about proper grooming as well. Giving him the right food is just a part of the whole process of keeping your dog as healthy as he can be.

Also by Lou Jefferson

Here are some of Lou Jefferson's other books. You can click on the covers to take a look at any of them.

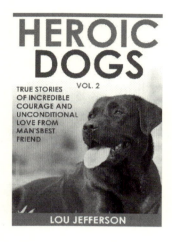

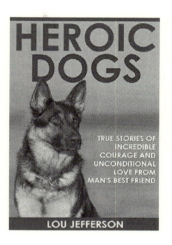

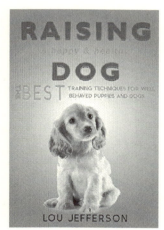

Made in the USA
Las Vegas, NV
17 November 2021